Quantum Leaps in Princeton's Place

Dr. Donna Clovis

BALBOA
PRESS
A DIVISION OF HAY HOUSE

Balboa Press books may be ordered through booksellers or by contacting:

Balboa Press
A Division of Hay House
1663 Liberty Drive
Bloomington, IN 47403
www.balboapress.com
1 (877) 407-4847

Print information available on the last page.

ISBN: 978-1-5043-2958-3 (sc)
ISBN: 978-1-5043-2959-0 (e)

Balboa Press rev. date: 04/13/2015

THIS BOOK IS DEDICATED TO JIM,
MATT, MICHAELA, AND JUSTIN

CONTENTS

FOREWORD

M y book title: *Quantum Leaps in Princeton's Place . . . How synchronicity helped me write a novel.*

I am a journalist. I had just won financial support from Harvard University and the American Council on Germany to document elderly Holocaust survivors in Germany back then. I found the elderly interesting to talk with. Now, I wanted to document the lives of some of the most elderly people living in Princeton, New Jersey, during the time my children attended Princeton Schools there. I felt that there must be such a wealth of knowledge in the community and university. I wanted to find out how much knowledge existed among the elderly.

I looked up the oldest living man and woman in Princeton at the time. I got in touch with them and asked them for an interview. The woman was one hundred years old. The man was one hundred three. Both were African American. I started to document their lives. Their interviews took six months. What was it like to live one hundred years ago in Princeton? There were so many famous people here: Albert Einstein, Paul Robeson, among others.

During the six months of interviews, my daughter had a play date with a new girl who attended her school. I traveled the road looking for the number on the house. We found ourselves driving down the driveway that led to a mansion. I asked my seven-year-old daughter, Michaela, "Are you sure your friend lives here?" And of course, she would not know. She was seven and this was the first time at the house.

We got out of the car and walked to the front door. Michaela rang the bell. When the door opened, her friend appeared with her mother.

The home was beautiful and large. They had just moved in and I could see the boxes piled within the first parlor. The mansion was old. She told me that it used to be a plantation house on many acres before it was later subdivided.

We sat down for tea while our children ran upstairs to play. "After tea, I want to give you a tour of the house," she told me, "It's historical. It has four floors with the top floors which used to be use as slave or maid quarters. Look what we found here."

She pulled out three boxes of old black and white photos from the early 1900s. They were pictures of the mansion when it was first built and the first owners. It was amazing to see. She then handed me a red journal.

"What is this?" I asked.

"It's a journal from Daisy. She was the first owner. She talks about how it was back then. She was an aristocrat. Knew a lot of famous people."

I started to read and read. And it hit me. I had been interviewing the oldest African Americans in the town. Was it possible? Were they here? So, I asked if she would not mind me borrowing the journal to read. "I promise. I'll bring it back tomorrow."

When I got home, I immediately called the people I was interviewing. He didn't know anything about the house, but she did. She grew up in the house and served as a maid.

When I returned to the house with the journal the next day, I told them what I found out. They told me to photocopy the journal. They said I could come at any time and write the novel in their house. I knew I had to write about this. I was in the right place at the right time. Synchronicity—a quantum leap in Einstein's town!

So, the hundred-year-old told me her story about her life as a child and woman in the house. I sat in the mansion from the garden and wrote. Another day, I sat in one of the parlors. Another day, I wrote from the slave quarters. I looked up historical records in periodicals of the time. I wrote and wrote until I was done.

I self-published the work as *Plantation* through Xlibris in 2000. I always felt that it was a story that was meant to be told.

Today, in 2015, I realized that the title should be changed. I renamed the book to *Quantum Leaps in Princeton's Place*. Being at the right place at the right time was inherent to writing the story! I'm looking to publish the book under this new name and add this as the Foreword since I own all rights. I realized how important this part was needed as the Foreword to the novel. Synchronicity!

CHAPTER 1

Rosedale Road in Princeton is treacherous when it rains. Dark and slick, water mixed with droplets of oil from cars, forms a baker's donut glaze on the surface of the wavy valley road. I travel this way often, in a champagne Mazda Protege stuffed like a shoe box with my daughter, Michaela, her friends, backpacks, pom poms, water bottles, and Ritz cheese snacks, driving them to classes and activities. It is the only road available from the top of the valley to Johnson Park School.

But today was unusual. Miss Ida B., a hundred-year-old woman living three houses down from us on John Street, called me to help with a few errands. Her grandchildren were out of town for the next few days. She needed diabetes medication from the pharmacy, some groceries, and a ride to the Princeton Cemetery, where a very close friend was being buried later that afternoon.

So Michaela wouldn't be bored with errands, I made arrangements for her to go home after school with a new friend who had just moved into the area on Rosedale Road.

"I'll pick up Michaela now and we'll have more than enough time to get you to the cemetery," I said, stopping the car at a traffic light.

Miss Ida B. looked out the window and sighed. "I just appreciate you doin' these errands for me, honey."

Miss Ida B., a large stately Black woman, dressed in black with a hat and veil that covered the tips of her eyebrows, is a mixture of empress and mother. Her expressive eyebrows arch high beneath her hat. When she smiles, her cheeks puff a bit, the wrinkles pull her face into a somber expression.

"I know the girl's mom said their house was before the school on the right," I said, searching both sides of the street. "These houses are mansions, Michaela couldn't be here."

Miss Ida B., whose large dark brown eyes luminesce like high-beam headlights whenever anything exciting happens, looked up. "I haven't been in this part of town for years," she said.

We drove into a long horseshoe-shaped driveway and parked next to a black Mercedes in front of a house. It was a New Jersey colonial-style mansion with massive gray stone and ivy-muffled brick, built on the second of five terraces that lead down the valley to a lake. The chimney belched forth smoke, impregnating the air with the scent of burning wood. It had four white columns that span across the front and a sweeping lawn with ancient trees.

"Rosedale," Miss Ida B. gasped. "I know this house."

"What did you say?" I rambled, taking off my seat belt. "I know, Michaela couldn't possibly be here, but I thought I better stop and ask."

Leaving the car running and Miss Ida B. in the front seat, I walked to the door. As I approached, looking upward at the imposing edifice, I noticed the mansion's intriguing design and character, like a human countenance. It had a heart, a pulse full of rich and somber remembrances.

There it rose in pride, withdrawn from the line of the road. I knocked and waited several minutes, but there was no answer. Thinking no one was home, I turned away and walked to the car.

"Wait," a voice cried from behind the large white door. "Wait, you must be Michaela's mom."

The door opened wide. A sudden gust of wind passed like a sigh. Anna Cronkite, a tall and slightly built woman in a bright yellow dress, pretty with high cheek bones and wide green eyes, appeared. "I'm sorry, it takes a while to get to the door since the house is so big. Come in," she said in a light gentle voice.

"The car's running and I have someone with me," I said, pointing to the car.

"No bother. Have her come inside too. The girls are watching videos in the upstairs playroom," Anna said gently.

I ran to the car and turned it off. I gently nudged Miss Ida B. on her shoulder. "Come inside. She's inviting us in for a moment. I don't want to leave you here," I said softly, opening a large orange and black umbrella to protect Miss Ida B. from the rain.

"Well, just for a few minutes," she said, standing. "I haven't seen the insides of this house in many years."

As we approached the front door, Anna greeted Miss Ida B. and smiled, "Hi!" I, in turn, introduced Miss Ida B. to Anna as we were ushered through the foyer.

"What a beautiful mansion," I remarked. "How old is it?"

"Oh, I know the housewarming was in 1912," Anna said. "It was originally built as a plantation house. Miss Daisy, a woman from Charleston, South Carolina, fell in

3

love with Princeton and had it built. The property originally overlooked fifty six acres of the valley."

The spacious entryway, with oriental rugs scattered throughout, opened into five large rooms. As regards its interior life, an old large mirror with golden trim hung in one of the rooms. It contained within its depths all souls reflected there. Two old portraits, surrounding a dark brown grandfather clock, were situated at the top of several stairs. The living room was a creamy beige, enhanced by Victorian furniture, brown sofa, and a black glossy Steinway in the corner. One of the rooms appeared to be a study with a narrow bookcase and small rug, but otherwise the house was virtually bare. The large windows and French doors looked out into dark green shrubbery.

Miss Ida B. peered at the rooms. "My, my," she started. "Nothing much has changed here. You still have the grandfather clock on the stairway, but this closet here. That used to be a telephone booth." She walked near the closet and looked it up and down.

"You know this house?" Anna asked with raised eyebrows.

"Uh, huh," Miss Ida B. began. "This house whispers so many memories. So many memories like a museum of the people who used to live here. Life flowed through these rooms. There were afternoon teas and dinner parties with skirts rustling across the wooden floors. Beethoven and Mozart mixed with soft voices. People have loved here, babies birthed here, death and spirits shuffled through these hallways. It was this house where I was trained for domestic work by my mother. It was this house where my mother was a servant."

"That's fascinating," said Anna excitedly. "We've just moved here. There's so much work to do and a lot of rooms are quite empty, but would you like to see the house? You could probably show me around. I'd be interested in some of your memories."

"I've got to get her to the Princeton Cemetery soon," I said, giving Miss Ida B. a hard glare.

Miss Ida B. smiled and nodded. "A few moments, dear. We have just enough time to see the second floor."

We followed Anna as she climbed the winding stairway to the second floor. An antique, white Carousel horse with red and gold reins, its nose snorting upward in front of a long row of windows, decorated the second floor landing.

"We'll start here first. I have the most beautiful view of the valley from the balcony in my bedroom." Anna said, opening the door.

The bedroom was simple. There was one double bed, with an orange flowered comforter, and two high-back orange chairs. A tall lush plant stood next to the bed. The pale walls were decorated with a single gold-framed painting of a countryside. The sun peered through French doors leading to the balcony.

"Wait until you see this!" Anna said, grabbing the door knobs and opening them simultaneously.

We followed Anna onto the peaceful privacy of a balcony, with plants draped over and clinging to the walls. The view was spectacular and the air was clear. Sprawling lawns, tailored court yards, and hills went on like infinity.

"Wow," I said, leaning over the balcony. "This is outrageous!"

"It's a little cool today," Anna said, shoving her hands down the neck of her shirt for warmth. "But we come out here often because it's breath-taking!" Anna smiled.

Miss Ida B. was quiet, almost trance-like. Taking a deep breath, she stared out into the valley. Miss Ida B. spoke in a soft voice, concentrating intensely, speaking in spurts and taking long pauses as she recalled the events of her childhood. "They used to call this Glen Gummere because of this valley's shape. The event I remember the most was the housewarming of Rosedale. I was only twelve then. I was helping Mama prepare the house and serve the guests. The servants were hustling the entire evening. We didn't have a chance to take a breath and rest. It was a very important day for Miss Daisy and her husband, Barker . . ."

CHAPTER 2

From a distance, it didn't look like an important event—a bunch of brown folding chairs on a large patio surrounded by vines and twisted thorn bushes. True, the guests were sitting on chairs, not really dressed-up people, but a torn teddy bear and two Raggedy Ann dolls. A sign on a makeshift post said "Welcome."

The Rosedale house was alive. Ida, a twelve-year-old girl with a thin flat body and ashy knees clothed in a black dress and white apron, stood in the spring afternoon sun on the upper landing of the second floor looking down at the patio. A slither of sunlight seeping through the dust caught her teeth flashed in a smile, her small nose, and her large brown eyes in the darkness of her face.

Suddenly, she spun around and grasped the edge of the railing. She raised her arm slowly and greeted the guests below. She imagined a crowd gathering around, fussing over her, she had become one of them. Ida threw her head back, her matted shoulder-length braids swayed a bit as she held up her imaginary black gown. Ida, at the top of the stairs, looked left then right, smiling dazzlingly. Then with deliberate dignity, she made the most of the moment and slowly descended down the staircase.

At the bottom of the stairs, near the potted plants on the patio, she paused and smiled at her guests. "I am so happy you were able to come," Ida said.

Suddenly the mood was broken. A voice bellowed through the doorway. "Ida, if you don' stop that daydreamin this minute, child!" yelled Carnethia Thomas, Ida's mother, as she wrestled folding chairs into place for the afternoon celebration. "Take your toys upstairs right away. It's Miss Daisy's housewarmin. This isn't the time!"

Ida's gown and imaginary crowd disappeared like Cinderella's dream at the stroke of midnight. She returned to her thin body, legs too long and arms flailing at her sides. Her dark face saddened as she looked down at the ground. Ida didn't belong here. She felt unholy in this sacred place. Everything was heavenly white, most of the walls, the columns, the walkways, the dishes, their faces. Ida and the servants seemed like dark shadows shifting through the lives of ghosts. Rosedale was their house. It was their party. These were their guests.

Carnethia, a tall woman with a strong lean body, hovered over Ida, casting a dark shadow. She brought a cool, stiff breeze like autumn across the patio. The sun hid behind the scattered clouds. Carnethia's mouth, with wrinkles drawn downward, implied little time for play. Her face always changed dramatically with her moods, perhaps the result of many difficult years. She placed her hands on her hips in protest. "Since you been here at Rosedale, you been like this, daydreamin. I want to make the best of this job. It's been the best job I had. We come too far. It's a nice clean house here, not the fields where I picked okra and butter beans under the hot Mississippi sun. I guess you don know bout that, do you?" Carnethia said irritably in a deep monotonous voice.

Ida's eyes dropped to her mother's feet. Suddenly, in one quick moment, Carnethia yanked one of Ida's matted braids, ripping away the white bow. "Answer me!" Carnethia scolded through clenched teeth.

Ida lifted her head, the sunlight glaring in her eyes, casting deep shadows from nearby tree branches across her body like prison bars. "No, Mama." She closed her eyes, wishing she was back home in Mississippi, running and playing free near the river.

"No, you young folk don know what that's like. Don care what that's like. And if you didn get up early enough, or you stopped your pickin cause you were hot from the sun beatin on your nappy hair and sweaty back, they whip you. Not once, but three four and five times. I ain goin back to that. You better straighten up. You hear?" Carnethia said severely with hand, poised mid-air to slap Ida's face.

They were alone in the kitchen now. Bare white walls listened.

Ida froze, but felt fiery hatred in the depths of her stomach. Carnethia lunged. A stinging slap cursed Ida's face. She flinched, but didn't move. Her mother's hand shook nervously inches from her face and slapped again. "Did you hear me?" Carnethia shouted, peering at Ida and sucking her teeth.

"Yes, Mama," Ida's voice quivered. She hated fighting like this. Ida feared her mother would kill her one day, but feared more the notion that someone would hear them, take her mother away or lock her up somewhere, and leave her alone in the Rosedale house to die.

"Get out of here, now. Get those toys off the patio. Miss Daisy's guests are due to arrive any moment," Carnethia muttered, blocking the entrance to the patio.

Ida whimpered, wiping the tears from her eyes, as she crouched low and squeezed through the dark opening between her mother and the doorway. The ghosts and the shadows grew silent. Ida ran quickly down the hallway and disappeared.

CHAPTER 3

In 1912, the Titanic was due to complete its voyage with a grand celebration on Pier 59 in New York City, but it didn't happened. Newspaper reporters wrote about horrific images and descriptions from survivors, the ship sinking sideways like a skyscraper spanning five New York City office blocks. The lights on the ship dimmed. There were several explosions underwater. Hundreds of voices called out across the cold vacant sea. Babies cried. A six-year-old survivor, Robert Spedder, and his family gave interviews. Stories of conspiracy and swindlers at work in Titanic lifeboats surfaced. Men held back tears. An eerie calm and the peaceful silence of death prevailed.

Everyone talked about the devastation of the "unsinkable ship," the one "God himself couldn't sink"—but something like a god, a powerful force of nature, an unfortunate mishap, nonetheless, a vivid bright flash woke up the world.

Titanic was the topic at the Rosedale's housewarming among the male guests to the dismay of Miss Daisy. She wanted them to notice her tasteful decorating and fine food, but they smoked cigars and talked about investments. They discussed America, Europe, immigration, history, and politics. And in between this, little by little, and reluctantly, tales about their lives. Smoke curled from their mouths and circled the air. Miss Daisy walked through their conversations several times, glancing at Barker Gummere, her husband, in a coy way.

Barker, a sturdily built man with a neatly trimmed mustache and brown thinning hair, caught the light beams from the sun in his distressed, green deep-set eyes. Sunlight spilled through the parlor windows and swayed to the music of Mozart. With pressed lips, Barker forcibly blew a stream of smoke high in the air and looked the other way in disdain. The topic was now current university lectures and the latest news about Woodrow Wilson's political aspirations.

Talk about Woodrow Wilson persisted in town. Two years earlier, Woodrow Wilson, then the president of Princeton University, argued with Dean Andrew West over the proposed building of a graduate school. Woodrow Wilson was vehemently opposed to such a rival building outside of his campus. The battle was so intense that dividing lines were formed and aligned throughout Princeton. People on opposing sides did not look at each other. They rarely spoke. Everyone gossiped. Dean West almost surrendered, but Mr. Isaac C. Wyman, a philanthropist, died leaving millions of dollars to Dean West for the building of his dreams, a graduate school.

The issue settled, Woodrow Wilson resigned as president of the university and went into politics. Now he was the Governor of New Jersey running for the office of President of the United States. Everyone was impressed.

While men spoke of politics, women whispered about women's rights away from the menfolk in other rooms. They spoke of Mary Philbrook, a tireless lawyer, who was fighting hard for voting rights. The National Suffrage League in New Jersey was soliciting the active support of women to march in parades and rallies.

Miss Daisy, with a southern drawl, led the discussion. She easily qualified as the type of woman some people considered strong-willed. Miss Daisy was never imposing— petite, slightly built, youthful for her twenty-seven years, and beautiful with wide blue eyes, high rosy cheeks, and a blonde upswept hairdo. But despite her elegant mannerisms and soft voice, she gave the impression of being a determined woman. "I just can't imagine participating in those things," said Miss Daisy, sipping a cup of tea. "It's just not proper."

"But we should have the right to vote," one woman whispered in a conspiratorial voice.

"We deserve rights," another woman nodded.

"But women, we have such fine lives without such a fuss," Miss Daisy explained with a delighted giggle. "Why, I wouldn't have the time to oversee my southern plantations, move all the way up here from Charleston, South Carolina, purchase this estate, build Rosedale, decorate my house, and have you over if I were marching in such parades. Besides Barker wouldn't hear of it." Miss Daisy smiled, wiping her brow with a handkerchief.

"Maybe," another woman hesitated.

"Maybe I'm right," Miss Daisy said and handed the tea cup and saucer to Carnethia who was standing nearby. "Now follow me, let me show you one more room before dinner is served. Since Princeton is filled with so many educated professionals, Barker and I thought our home would not be complete without a well-appointed library." Daisy gave a vehement gesture with her hands. Then in a

13

flurry of words, spoken in a high tone, she described her choice of decor as she led the group into the room.

The library was Barker's haven, ceiling to floor with books and overstuffed with two desks, two cabinets with glass tops, three lamps with red metal lamp shades, and two spindle-back chairs that sat at opposite ends of the fireplace. There were fancy paintings in heavy gold frames hanging on the walls. Knick-knacks, given as presents by aunts and uncles from the South, covered the coffee table in the corner, and a lush embroidered red velvet curtain swept across the back window, looking out to the patio.

"It just took forever to decorate this," Miss Daisy said, running her fingers across a red velvet plush chair.

"It's beautiful," one woman admired.

"A library with a fireplace," another woman commented. "How impressive."

At that moment, Carnethia appeared in the doorway. "Miss Daisy, ma'am. Supper is about ready, if you wouldn't mind comin into the dining room," Carnethia said softly, wiping the sweat from her brow.

"Thank you, Carnethia," Miss Daisy smiled. "We have a European-style banquet, a celebratory treat awaiting you. If you all wouldn't mind following me to the dining room."

The ornate dining room with stained glass and two fireplaces had a large golden chandelier suspended from the center of the ceiling. The room was filled with decorative art in frames, sculptures, and blue velvet tapestries. A long communal table awaited them, decked in a white linen tablecloth with the finest china, silver, and glassware. Pink roses waited patiently next to each white plate. Goblets of red wine and glasses of water were filled to the brim.

Several servants scurried pass the guests with sourdough breads, fruits, appetizers of coconut shrimp with thatches of sugarcane, green beans, carrots, noodles, and five large turkeys. Apple tarts and chocolates waited in the kitchen for dessert.

Armed with tireless jaws, thirty-six people were seated for the feast. Others treated themselves to the informal buffet served on platforms on the second terrace. Among the guests were John Greer Hibben, later president of Princeton University, Mr. and Mrs. Taylor Pyne, who sent a wagon of flowers from their greenhouse, Mrs. Woodrow Wilson, and others from Princeton, Trenton, New York, Charleston, and New Orleans.

Miss Daisy, with her two main ambitions: being thought of well by Princeton University wives and acceptance into the prestigious Present Day Club, placed Mrs. Katherine Cosby Warren, its president and her husband, Howard, Princeton's first psychology professor, next to her at the dining table. Miss Daisy was the first to pass along the sourdough bread. "Try it," she said to Katherine. "My servants are wonderful cooks."

"No, thank you," Katherine said politely, raising her nose in the air. "I don't care for sourdough breads, but I'd love to try the shrimp."

Miss Daisy beckoned Carnethia, with the snap of her finger, from across the table. "Quickly please, Katherine would like shrimp. Please gather a platter and serve her."

"Yes, ma'am," Carnethia nodded.

Those sitting closest to Katherine and Howard, paying attention, created a ripple effect, picking out food that looked good on their plates.

The servants provided platters like magicians, making empty dishes disappear and tasty foods reappear.

Katherine did not say much as they dined. Miss Daisy tried to mirror her manners, smiling nervously between bites. Unimpressed, Katherine glanced up and away. Her gaze did not shift during dinner or dessert, neither did her head turn from its obstinate angle, but remained stressed.

At the conclusion of dessert, Mr. James Alexander, one of the trustees of Princeton University, and Barker read original poetry. Music of Beethoven played muted in the background while groups posed for portraits in the parlor. Two Rose family photographers stood by their tripods with their heads hidden beneath black cloth. Some danced the reel at midnight. As Barker and Miss Daisy came down the middle, they whispered how thankful they were for Rosedale.

That evening, the sun set deep red against a blue slate sky, then darkened black like a silhouette portrait. Under the night, Rosedale finally rested and each lighted window twinkled and extinguished itself good-night.

CHAPTER 4

It was a sure sign of spring as daffodils and daisies themselves—an ice cream truck chugged down Witherspoon Street, crooning a call of carnival songs that sent anyone under the age of twelve and some older folk scurrying to buy a creamy taste of heaven.

Beautiful dark girls in bright-colored bonnets and young boys in gray suits, with fingers meshed in the hands of their parents, strolled home from church services. It was the custom for families to spend Sunday afternoons gathered on porches, chatting with neighbors and those passing by. Grandmothers, dressed in their Sunday best with fans in hand, sat on white porches in rocking chairs. Sunday was a day of rest. God gave colored folk the day off.

It was the day after the Rosedale housewarming and Ida was excited to escape her mother and the mansion to be with friends. Ida climbed the stairs to the front porch of her best friend's house on John Street and knocked on the door. Florence Smith, a fourteen-year-old, dark-skinned girl with wide eyes and smile, opened the door. She was three inches taller and towered above Ida's head. Her small breasts nudged the inside of her pink blouse as she brushed buster-brown bangs away from her face. "How was the housewarmin party?" Florence asked.

"I hated it," Ida complained. "I helped Mama work the whole time."

"I'm sorry," Florence said softly. "Yesterday my Mama and Papa took us to New York City for the first time. It was wonderful." Florence, who didn't use two words when fifty were available, delivered a chatty, sentimental description of New York City. Clapping her hands, she turned and whirled in a long black skirt and white ankle socks. "We even saw the likes of a night club where people were dancin."

When Florence opened the front door wider, a round-face boy appeared bouncing on the edge of the sofa. Timmy Smith, Florence's seven-year-old brother, had never met any furniture he didn't want to jump on. The sofas and chairs in the living room, like sinking ships, were torn, and there were no chairs in the dining room. Florence pointed to her aunt's wedding photograph trimmed in silver on the table. "That's the way this house looked before Timmy. We're gettin used to be comfortable on the floors."

"Will your Mama let you go downtown?" Ida asked excitedly.

"Yes, let me go upstairs and get some money," Florence said as she disappeared upstairs. She quickly raced downstairs. "Now I'm ready."

Ida and Florence strolled from Witherspoon Street to Nassau Street. They passed the stone and black iron-grille fence like a castle fortress that buffered the quiet green courtyards and walkways of the inner sanctuary at Princeton University from the bustling business area of town. The turbulence of Nassau Street, with cars, voices, horse-drawn buggies, and trolleys, persisted. University students and townsfolk bore down upon store windows of Waterford and Lenox. The peacefulness of grass and thick trees across the street never shuddered, but observed the commotion in silence.

"Let's cut through here," Florence said, grabbing Ida's arm.

"Mama said we can't cut through the university," Ida reminded.

"Oh, hush. I've done it plenty times. And no one says nothin," Florence said, fixing her braids. "Follow me."

The girls walked along twisted paths in an atmosphere of calm and divinity between tall, looming stone buildings thick with ivy. Hand in hand, Ida felt a sense of happiness and freedom she never experienced at Rosedale. For a moment, life had changed. The large trees shielded two dark little girls from the rest of the world in their shade. Intoxicated with freedom and humming "Swing Low Sweet Chariot," they skipped through Princeton University's courtyards. A gust of wind whipped through their legs and rustled their flowered dresses. Suddenly, Florence stopped and grabbed Ida's arm.

"Shhh," she said. "Look over here."

"What?" Ida complained.

"Shhh," she said as she peeked around the building. "Look, they're kissing, I think"

On the hill lay a man and a woman, embraced as one on a brown blanket in the grass. Their mouths were intact and their bodies sunk deep within each other.

"I don't care." Ida protested.

"But if you watch long enough . . . they may be doing something else," Florence explained.

"What do you mean? Do something else like what?" Ida asked.

"Shhh, they're goin to get up and run away," Florence said, covering Ida's mouth.

"What do you mean?" Ida whispered, removing Florence's hand from her mouth.

"You know. . . . Didn't your Mama tell you?"

There were several grunts and a wild shout.

"That. We missed it 'cause of you." Florence said, placing her hands on her hips.

"Missed what?"

"You're hopeless. Your Mama needs to talk to you."

"My Mama don tell me nothin," Ida said pushing Florence. "Now catch me if you can!"

Ida raced away from Florence and the lovers on the hill. Out of breath, Ida paused at the iron-grille fence, pulling her white socks out of the back of her black shoes. "I told you. I'm too fast for you." Ida said. "We better get out of here before we get into trouble."

As Ida and Florence walked down Nassau Street towards the Rosedale House, they heard the rising chants of their names behind them.

Thinking that she was in trouble, Ida began to run through the crowded sidewalk. "Wait!" Florence yelled, grabbing Ida's arm. "What are you runnin for? You're such a fraidy cat."

Turning, Ida saw two boys and two girls waving at her. They were her classmates from the Witherspoon School for the Colored. "You missed a great movie," a boy, with rough hair parted to the side, said.

"It was pretty good," another boy said.

"I don't like sittin in the back. I can't see from the back," Ida complained. "Then if you can't see, why go to the stupid movie?"

Florence rubbed the back of Ida's neck. Something in Florence soothed her and calmed her anger. "We had more fun than you in that dark movie house," Florence teased. "We saw two real people. Two real people lyin on each other. We watched them."

"Hush," Ida shoved Florence. "We did not. We just took a nice walk."

The boys and girls looked at each other and giggled at Ida as if she was left out of a secret. "Hey, wanna go to the candy store?" a boy asked.

"Sure," Ida smiled. "But I have to walk home and get some money. Wanna walk home with me to Rosedale? Then I can go."

They strolled slowly from Nassau Street to the Rosedale house, like a dark sea creeping its way along a pale, sandy beach. As Ida knocked and entered the large foyer at Rosedale, the sunlight spilled upon the white walls and a gentle breeze blew the chandelier hanging from the ceiling, sending rainbow lights across dark faces. "I ain never seen anythin like this," one boy said. "You really live here?"

"Yes, me and Mama live here, but way upstairs in the servant's quarters. It don't look anythin like this. I'd rather like where you all live on John Street. You have nicer houses and friends around. It gets lonely," Ida said. "You better wait down here. I've got to ask Mama for a nickel."

But Ida could already feel her mother's presence as she came downstairs. The expression on her face and strong stride reprimanded Ida before she spoke.

"Mama, can I have a nickel for the candy store?" Ida asked.

"I reckon you think you and this group are going somewhere?" her mother asked, placing her hands on her hips.

"Yes, Mama," Ida paused uncomfortably as her eyes dropped to the ground. "I need a nickel for the candy store."

"You know I don let you out of this house with boys. What you think you grown now and can go off datin without permission?" Carnethia said, clenching her teeth. "Now say good day to your friends."

As Ida's friends left the front door, Carnethia's arm rose high to hit Ida's face. "Now who are those boys?"

"They just from school, Mama. We weren't doing anything. I just wanted candy," Ida begged.

Carnethia pounced and slapped Ida. She seized Ida's white collar and brought her close to her face. "I don't believe you," Carnethia shouted.

"But Mama," Ida pleaded.

"But Mama nothin. You don listen. I can't have you gettin in trouble. I don want trouble with these boys and most of all trouble with these white folk. You know, they think we stupid anyhow. And you hangin out with boys will raise some brows around here. I ain raisin no whoe, understand?" Carnethia's dark finger trembled close to Ida's face.

Ida trembled.

"Now get over there and close that front door so folk don hear me," Carnethia said bluntly.

Ida closed the front door.

"Get out of here," Carnethia said, throwing Ida's small body against the white wall with a loud thud.

The rainbow lights from the chandelier disappeared. The glimmering sunlight was now hidden behind the front door. Ida lay sprawled on the polished wooden floor. Stunned, she rose to her feet and ran upstairs sobbing.

CHAPTER 5

The next Saturday morning at dawn, Miss Daisy and Barker lay in bed in their fairy tale bedroom, framed with pink and white ruffled curtains. The sunlight sliced through the bedroom window and cut a single strip across Barker's hunched body. Miss Daisy's long blonde hair was undone and lay about her face on the yellow flowered pillow case. Barker groped for her, his hands rotating on her nipples. She found his hand and pressed it hard on her breasts and guided his hand down her flank between her thighs, begging for his thrusts. Full passion broke out and the bed rippled like the ocean, then calmed like a passing storm at sea.

Barker opened the curtains and let the morning sun into the bedroom. Miss Daisy sat up and covered both eyes with her hands. "Oh, Barker. I continue thinking about our housewarming last weekend. Did you enjoy it as much as I did?" Miss Daisy said with her arm perched on the end table beneath her chin.

"It was quite nice," Barker said softly.

"I'm just amazed at how many Southerners live in this town. I think there's more people from the South living in Princeton than Northerners. It makes for a quaint atmosphere, don't you think?" Miss Daisy said, brushing her long blonde hair, looking in the mirror.

"The professors I've spoken to from the university seem to agree with you. They say as early as 1840, slave owners owed much of their liking of Princeton to the faculty's conservative politics and the advocacy of the African colonization movement instead of the abolition of slavery. This made our town the perfect political place for Southerners to live. I believe the university's student attendance peaked with more Southerners than Northerners in the same year. Princeton has a southern charm that has drawn many people like us from North Carolina, South Carolina, Mississippi, and Louisiana. It's quite ironic," he said, rubbing his face long and hard.

"Is that what you men talked about last week?" Miss Daisy said, her blue eyes widening.

"Hardly," he murmured, stroking her arm. "We talked mostly of investments."

"Everyone seemed to have a nice time, but Mrs. Katherine, the club's president. I received a gracious thank you from everyone but her. Nothing seems to stir that woman. I don't know how I'll get her attention. That President's Club is the most prestigious club in Princeton and I must get in," Miss Daisy said with a persistent voice.

Barker's laughter twisted the air. "I don't think you have a chance, Daisy. The woman didn't give you any attention. I don't think she was impressed."

This infuriated Miss Daisy and rage welled up in her face, turning it red. "It's not funny. Acceptance by university women is important in this town. You are nothing without them!" she shouted.

His hollow laughter rose higher as he walked across the room. "You put too much importance on these women and they know it. That's why they elude you," Barker said.

"I declare, Barker. You just don't understand," Miss Daisy said, folding her arms across her chest.

Barker gave her the usual grimace and shrug. "I just don't want to see you hurt," he said as he came closer, placing his hand on her shoulder.

Her eyes narrowed. "And it seems to me you have no problem with the university men or women. You have three invitations to their clubs next week without me. Besides, Christine Boyd, Professor Angus's wife, had so much to say to you."

He wet his lips, saying nothing.

"Answer me," Miss Daisy demanded, standing.

Barker avoided her eyes as he dressed. "Christine just adores the house, Daisy," he reassured her. "As usual, you're overreacting. You're feelings are hurt because of Katherine. Don't let her upset you. We have a wonderful place here at Rosedale. More than she will ever have," Barker leaned over and kissed her cheek.

"Where are you going?" Miss Daisy asked.

"Over to the university," Barker said. "I have some errands to run. And Professor Angus wants theater tickets. As president of the Trenton Theater Company, I can't let him down. You know that's not good for business. I promise not to be long."

Miss Daisy sighed and slammed her brush on the bureau. "I wanted to see if we could stop by Mrs. Wilson's to see her gardens," she said irritably.

"Has she invited us?" Barker asked, raising his left brow.

"Why no, I just thought if she saw us passing by, we could . . . " Miss Daisy started, flashing her blue eyes.

"No, Daisy," Barker said abruptly. "I don't believe in forcing my way on people. Now I'll be back in a few hours. We have the theater in Philadelphia this evening to look forward to. Maybe you can visit the Taylor's new hotel in Trenton. Do a little shopping while you're there. You've been wanting to visit. Now you have some time," Barker smiled as he closed the bedroom door.

Miss Daisy arrived at the hotel in Trenton, a beautiful red-brick building on State Street, later that morning. The air was crisp and clear with hazy white sunlight. The clatter of horse and buggies, automobile horns, and the clanking of trolleys surrounded her. Noisy voices swirled through the air. A dark-skinned man tap-danced for a crowd on the opposite corner. Miss Daisy ambled around, peering wistfully through neighboring store windows. She admired two women in peach bonnets and hoop skirts, clustered into large bouquets, standing for their portrait outside a store.

As she approached the hotel, she was greeted by a doorman who escorted her into the lobby. The lobby was beautiful, with dark wood walls, carved ceilings, and blue tapestries. A large chandelier, suspended in the center, glowed like a jewel in twilight. The lights cast their gaze in all directions including the walls.

"I'm here to see the Taylors," Miss Daisy told the doorman.

"Certainly," he said, peering through his thick steel-rimmed spectacles. "Take the elevator down this corridor to the fifth floor. Their suite is number 500."

It was only a few moments before the elevator arrived to take Miss Daisy upstairs. "Good morning, ma'am," the elevator operator said as the door opened.

"Good morning," Miss Daisy smiled as she stepped into the small elevator compartment. Suddenly, Miss Daisy tripped getting into the elevator. The operator, seeing her fall, let go of the lever to pick her up. The elevator car leaped into violence. It rushed up with Miss Daisy's body prone on the floor and both legs outside the car.

"Help me, for God's sake, stop the elevator!" she cried.

The operator got up quickly and reached for the lever, stopping it just in time to prevent the amputation of both legs. One leg was cut to the bone and the other was crushed and broken.

"Help!" the elevator operator screamed into the dark corridor. "Help, there's been an accident!"

Distress filled Miss Daisy's eyes, her head bowed. She raised her eyes, crying to the point of exhaustion and laid her head down again. The elevator operator stood above her. His tall lean shadow blocked the light and brought a sudden darkness into the elevator. He knelt and embraced her. "It will be all right, Miss. Help is on the way. Help is on the way," he tried to reassure her.

She moaned and the room went black.

Miss Daisy was rushed immediately to the local hospital where she lay in plaster for the next three months. The hospital was cold and institutional-looking, with white walls and tiles in dim electric light. Her hospital room, a small cool room chaste white like a convent, soon became a floral display, smelling of roses and carnations. Barker spent many evenings by her side. Numerous friends visited to cheer her, never coming empty-handed.

When Barker brought Miss Daisy home from the hospital, she was pleasantly surprised by dinners served by club waiters and opera singers who entertained. Except for the bandages on both legs, Miss Daisy was no different. She had the same wide blue eyes, smile, and spirit of determination.

Every afternoon at 5:00 in the drawing room, where Barker put Miss Daisy's makeshift bed and end table, women friends, shoppers, and business men gathered to see her. She kept up with the latest news, current events, and gossip. She listened to the best heated political discussions in town. Most acquaintances, friends, and relatives came, with the exception of Katherine and other university women. Some said they were quite busy this time of year and certainly sent their regards.

Soon Miss Daisy was out and about again, but she never walked the same, needing the assistance of a cane for balance. Her first agenda was contacting Katherine and the university women for a house party. Miss Daisy had missed them so.

CHAPTER 6

Carnethia, hunched in prayerful meditation over the stove in the servant's quarters, slowly poured hot water onto the freshly cut collard greens in a pot. After turning on the back burner, she blended eggs, milk, sugar, and corn meal in a large ceramic bowl. Carnethia beat the mixture in a syncopated rhythm until she broke into a sweat. Wiping her brow, she sighed and placed the batter in a sizzling black skillet filled with hot oil. The small kitchen swelled with heat. Puffs of smoke chugged through a crack between the lid and pot of collard greens like a locomotive. Carnethia opened the oven to check the nearly done cake. Today was Ida's thirteenth birthday.

Ida walked slowly into the kitchen and curled up on a chair in the corner beneath the caged sunlight. Her face was gray and drawn. Pain crept into the depths of her hips and lower back. "I don't feel so good, Mama," Ida complained.

"It's somethin you get used to. You're growin up into a woman now. You'll have those aches and pains now. It's just the third month, it should lighten up for you one of these months soon," Carnethia explained as she removed the cake from the oven to cool and then sat down beside her. "Soon you'll be thinkin of men and wantin to get married and . . ."

"I want to go to college," Ida sat up a little. "I want to be a teacher. I want to teach children how to read and write. I don't want to clean people's houses for the rest of my life."

Carnethia's head snapped up immediately as she jumped from the table, abandoning the chitterlings she was cleaning. Carnethia hushed Ida with a hard look. "Are you sayin I'm nothin cause I clean houses? Are you sayin you goin to be better than me? If it weren't for me and my work, you'd be nothin and nowhere. Do you understand?" Carnethia whispered through clenched teeth.

"Mama, no. I respect your work, but I want to do somethin else," Ida raised her voice.

"Now are you sassin me?" Carnethia raised her hand to slap Ida.

"No, Mama, please," Ida begged.

"Good then," Carnethia lowered her hand slowly. "Good, I didn't think you'd be sassin me feelin the way you do."

Ida lowered her eyes. "Mama, I don't feel well. Maybe cold water will help. Can I have a glass of cold water?" Ida whined with a look of anguished despair as she slumped against the kitchen window.

"No, not cold water. Hot tea. Hot tea is better for you," Carnethia said, putting on a pot of water.

"But I'm already sweatin," Ida complained putting her head on the table.

Carnethia turned, frowning. "It will make you sweat more," she said stepping toward Ida.

Her mother was standing in front of her now. Carnethia's yellow flowered dress smelled of Sunday perfume. Ida tried to avoid her mother's stare. She looked up and away through the window. A feeling of fear welled up inside her.

"My, look at you," Carnethia said softly, gently lifting Ida's chin. "Stand up, child."

Ida stood up slowly, her small breasts nudging the inside of her yellow blouse as she leaned against the kitchen table.

"You a woman now," Carnethia smiled, understanding. "Right before my eyes you turnin into a woman." She hugged Ida.

Ida listened, her dark brown eyes staying fixed upon her mother.

"I'll make you hot tea. It will make you feel better. And I have your favorite chocolate cake for your birthday," Carnethia said, rubbing the top of Ida's hair.

A silence gathered between them in the kitchen for dinner. They ate collard greens, corn bread, and chitterlings. Carnethia sang "Happy Birthday" and Ida made a wish for a boy. The gray smoke from thirteen candles ascended and disappeared into the white walls.

CHAPTER 7

The next Sunday afternoon, rain came down cold and steady. A gust of wind scattered a few crumbled gum wrappers across the front lawn of the Princeton YMCA. In the heavy mist, one could hardly see the silhouettes of people streaming into the building from the street.

Ida and Florence shot up the sidewalk, dodging puddles like fighter pilots. Tight, wet curls contoured their faces beneath the hoods of their pea-green raincoats. As Florence opened the door for Ida, they ran into Miss May, a woman nearly as old as a century with gray pressed hair, draped in a red coat, sitting next to the entrance like a queen. "And how are you, younguns, this miserable afternoon?" she asked, grabbing Ida's hand.

"Fine. Thank you, ma'am," Ida said politely.

Florence nodded vigorously, trying to get away, but it was too late. Miss May recalled a favorite memory about her youth. "Back down South, when I was your age, I just couldn't wait to spend time with my friends, hiding behind the cornstalks when we were supposed to be pickin cotton. And we'd laugh and talk and look for boys. I'm a little too old for that now," she chuckled, then gasped and coughed.

Florence noticed a few classmates hovered over a checkerboard in the back of the crowded room. "Good day to you, Miss May," she said, grabbing Ida's arm as they squeezed through the maze of dark faces toward their friends.

"Thanks for savin me," Ida smiled.

"I thought we'd be there all day," Florence laughed. "If it weren for me, you'd still be standin there."

Ida, behind Florence, paused when she approached Beatrice and four girls at one of the checker tables. "Mama said I'm not supposed to be talkin with Beatrice," Ida warned.

"Mama's not here," Florence whispered. "And so what can Beatrice do in a room full of people at the Y anyway?" Florence said, putting her hands on her hips.

Ida glared at Florence, shrugging her shoulders with a loose-limbed, clumsy grace. "I don't know," she whispered. "I don't care."

"Ida, Florence," Beatrice said, looking up from the checker table. "Look, I'm beatin Pam over here. King me! I won! I won! This is the third game today and I've beat her every time. Anyone else want to play me?" Beatrice bragged.

The crowd of girls surrounding the small table shook their heads from side to side. "Not me," Pam said in a tone of indifference, leaving the table. "I've had enough."

"Wait," Beatrice grabbed Pam's hand. "I've got somethin to tell you."

Pam slowly sat down again. "This better be good," she said.

"Remember that cute boy I met three weeks ago here? The one that comes by to see me nearly every day?" Beatrice whispered, leaning across the table.

"Yea," Pam said. "So?"

Beatrice sat back, crossing her legs and adjusting the straps of her dress. Then, with a slight nod, she sighed. The table became silent. Ida, Florence, and three girls hovered above Beatrice and Pam in deep concentration, taking everything in like a sponge.

Beatrice, the fifteen-year-old girl who had spoken, was brown-skinned and thin with rough carved features, red lipstick, and unkempt nappy hair. She wore a long green dress with the battered high-lace black shoes and sagging white socks of poor children. Beatrice lived on Baker Street, with the curtains in her house always drawn. Some said it was to hide the peeling flowered wallpaper, the chandelier with one working bulb, and tattered green couches in her living room. Ida's mother disapproved of Beatrice not because she was of little means, but because she managed to skip school, smoke, and avoid homework.

"And?" Florence asked abruptly.

"And we were in my house last week. My Mama always has to work, so she wasn't home. And we started kissin and kissin some more," Beatrice teased.

"You didn't," Pam shook her head from side to side.

"And we turned out the lights. And he said he loved me," Beatrice continued with wide eyes. "Wait, I've got to have a cigarette. Come on outside in the back and I'll tell you more."

The girls followed Beatrice out the back door of the YMCA. They huddled beneath the ledge of the roof, away from the rain. Beatrice took a cigarette from her pocketbook and lit it. Concentrating intensely, she spoke in spurts with long pauses as she selected her words. "And he told me he loved me again and he loved me so much he wanted to marry me." Beatrice ranted, sucking on her cigarette.

"But you're only fifteen," Ida complained.

Another girl snickered. "So how does he kiss?" she asked.

Beatrice took another drag on her cigarette, smiled, and fiddled with her nappy hair for a moment. "And I never had anyone tell me they loved me before. It was the most wonderful feelin."

"Oh, my," Ida looked away and shrugged in embarrassment.

"Did your Mama catch you?" Pam asked in shock.

"Did his kiss feel good?" another girl asked with a scrutinizing glance, impatiently fiddling with her long black braids.

"Yeah, it was great," Beatrice smiled. "It was the best feelin I ever had. And I didn't even get caught."

Ida covered her mouth in disbelief and horror. Her mother warned her about sinning like this, staying out all night with boys and smoking. Suddenly, Ida tugged on Florence's shoulder. "We better get inside," she said cautiously. "We're startin to smell like Beatrice's cigarette. My Mama's goin to think I've been smokin and I don't want to get a whippin."

Florence followed Ida inside as Beatrice gave full details of her escapade. "I wanted to hear more," Florence whined. "You just don want to grow up, do you?"

"It's my Mama," Ida said, stunned with rage. "You don't know what it's like to live with my Mama. My Mama won't let me grow up. If I try to grow up, she whips me, but my body's growing up and my mind is growin up and I'm a child living in that big old house by myself with my Mama. I hate this," Ida started to cry.

"I'm sorry," Florence hugged Ida. "I'm sorry. Really, I am. I know you have a tough Mama. I know. I know."

Ida sobbed on Florence's shoulder more.

"Shhhh," Florence tried to quiet Ida. "There's people lookin and they might ask what's wrong. Dry up your tears now. Quickly."

Ida wiped her hands across her wet eyes. "I'm all right."

"Look," Florence pointed to an empty table with a checkerboard. "Let's play. I bet I can beat you."

"No you can't," Ida tried to smile.

"Let's see. Try me," Florence said as she sat down.

Ida sat across from Florence and set up the red checkers. "Your move," her voice quivered.

The noise of the crowd at the Y, shooting pool, playing cards, talking, laughing, and the aroma of barbecue, engulfed them. Ida, with her head bowed, gazed at the black and red squares on the checkerboard, contemplating her next move.

CHAPTER 8

The extreme winter months blanketed everything white. A few dangling leaves, covered with frost's shimmer, glistened in the sunlight. The wind blew. Carnegie Lake froze. A white flag, placed in front of the Lower Pyne building on Witherspoon and Nassau, signaled the ice was solid and safe. On weekends, there was the constant sound of silver blades crisscrossing on the ice. Couples held hands. Children with flailing scarves darted between older ones. The elderly used old chairs with runners, their tracks quickly erased precious moments of the past.

Miss Daisy, with red checks and nose, wore a long brown coat with a fur hat and muff. Barker patiently held her arm. It was first time Miss Daisy put on skates since the accident and she was quite wobbly and unsure. "I declare, Barker," she said with a grin. "I thought this would be easier."

"Just don't try so hard," Barker said seriously. "We don't need another accident."

"Oh, Barker," Miss Daisy paused and looked. "Miss Katherine's here! I want to talk to her." Miss Daisy struggled free from Barker's arm.

Miss Katherine, a robust woman with a long black coat and hat, took solemn strides on the ice with her head bowed. Miss Daisy tried to get her attention as she skated by.

"Miss Katherine," Miss Daisy waved as she attempted to keep up with her. "Wait!"

Miss Katherine greeted Miss Daisy with a polite coolness. Then with her eyes fixed indifferently ahead, she skated away without a word. Barker followed close behind and grabbed Miss Daisy around the waist. "I told you to stop chasing that woman," Barker said flatly. "I want you to have a good time."

"But I was only trying to say hello," Miss Daisy pleaded. "I wanted to invite her to a house party."

"She hasn't accepted any invitations except the housewarming," Barker complained. "Why do you think she will accept an invitation now?"

Miss Daisy's voice dropped. "I know, but she's a very busy woman . . ."

Barker gave her the usual grimace and shrug. "Look, over there," Barker pointed. "It's Professor Angus and Christine. Come on," he said, holding Miss Daisy's hand.

Professor Angus was a calm man, almost plodding. He peered over his thick spectacles. "Good day, Barker. Lovely day for skating, isn't it?"

"It's beautiful," Barker spoke thoughtfully. "I think we're a little cold. Would you like to join us for hot chocolate at Renwick's?"

Christine glanced at Barker and smiled. She pulled her thick, shoulder-length red hair back and dropped it as she giggled. Her melodious, high-pitched voice had the drawl of an upper-class English woman. "I'd love some hot chocolate. I'm terribly cold now."

"Wonderful," Barker spoke rapidly. "I'll save a table and we'll meet you there in a few minutes."

At Renwick's Ice Cream and Soda Water Parlor on Nassau Street, a crowd had already gathered. The line spilled outside the restaurant onto the sidewalk. "I was afraid of this," Miss Daisy said, waving her cane. "Everyone wants hot chocolate at the same time."

Barker paused. "Professor Angus and Christine are coming," he said.

Professor Angus and Christine huddled behind them in line. "Looks like we have a wait," Professor Angus chuckled, taking his spectacles off and on absentmindedly.

"Renwick's has the best hot chocolate," Barker started, arching an eyebrow almost audibly at Christine. "I watched you skate. You skate very well. Did you have lessons?"

"Why, when I was a little girl, I took lessons, but I haven't practiced in a while," Christine smiled shyly.

"You're wonderful," Barker complimented.

Miss Daisy gave Barker a penetrating look.

"Oh, Daisy. It's so good to see you up and about skating. Why after that terrible accident, it's a miracle you can walk," Christine said in a warm and friendly tone.

Miss Daisy remained poised. "Yes, it's quite a blessing to be up and about."

"You must come visit sometime," Christine said with a grin. "Angus and Barker have developed such a friendship."

Miss Daisy looked away. "Yes, Barker should give your husband a rest," she said sarcastically. "I would think he's getting tired of having him drop by so often."

The sun hid behind clouds, turning the sky gray. The wind blew harder. Christine squirmed and looked at Angus. "Dear, it's awfully cold out. Must we wait so long? Perhaps we should go home," Christine whispered.

"Perhaps," Professor Angus said, looking up at the sky. "It has gotten quite chilly out here. Barker, maybe we will take you up on hot chocolate another time."

"Yes, Barker. I'm quite chilly also and this line doesn't seem to be moving," Miss Daisy said, with intense concern.

"You are right. Hot chocolate doesn't seem like a good idea today. It is awfully cold. But Professor Angus, before we leave, I have more theater tickets for next weekend in Philadelphia. Would you and Christine care to join us?" Barker asked politely.

"I must check my schedule," Professor Angus said, fidgeting with his spectacles. "We love theater. I'm certain that we'd love to go if we have nothing planned."

The couples departed. Miss Daisy walked in silent bitterness, arm in arm with Barker. He glanced at his gold pocket watch. It was 4:00 in the afternoon. The sky had darkened. A brisk wind blew. Snow flurries like powder sifted through the air.

CHAPTER 9

The sun shone brightly late Sunday afternoon over the maple trees and bushes surrounding the Princeton YMCA. Fragrances of barbecued chicken and corn bread seeped through the air. Music played. Little boys danced with their sisters. Old men tapped their feet.

Thomas, a fastidiously groomed sixteen-year-old with black curly hair, stood behind the Princeton YMCA in the shadows of the summer sun. His arms wrapped tightly around Ida's waist. He rested his lips against the softness of her cheek, then caught her mouth as she tried to turn away.

"That's enough," Ida protested. "Someone's going to catch us out here."

"I've been seeing you for three months now and we've never kissed. We've gotten close, but that's all," Thomas whispered in her ear, gently nibbling. His hands caressed her hair as his lips brushed pass Ida's closed eyes.

Suddenly, his mouth opened to hers. She stiffly accepted his kiss. He pressed harder and the warmth from their mouths melted inward. It was like taking a swig of gin on a hot summer afternoon at Beatrice's house. It was the same swooning sensation throughout her head and body.

Her arms dropped to her sides. "My Mama's going to kill me," she chuckled, glancing at his eyes quickly.

"Your Mama doesn't have to know," Thomas grinned, trying to kiss her again. "You're pretty good for the first time."

Ida smiled. "Not again, Thomas," she turned away. "I want to, but someone's bound to come out here now and catch us."

Thomas paused, thinking. "Then let's leave, no one's home at my house." He pulled her arm like a child tugging brusquely at a toy wagon.

"But I told Mama I'd be here. Besides, I came with Florence and she'll be looking for me," Ida said, withdrawing.

"Then a short walk. How about a short walk to the park? We won't be long," Thomas said.

"I don't know," Ida hesitated.

"We won't be long. No one will miss us. I promise," Thomas said, grabbing her hand.

"All right. Just a few minutes, you hear? You're bound to get me in trouble yet," Ida grinned.

They walked apart in silence for a long time until they found a park bench nestled between trees. A gentle wind blew through the leaves like a sigh. The sunlight illuminated Ida's face. They sat close on the bench, not touching. Thomas's laughter finally broke the stillness. "I can't believe we've gotten away," he chuckled. "Did I ever tell you that you are beautiful?"

Ida averted his glance. "No, you haven't," she said shyly.

"I'm saying it to you now," Thomas said, embracing her. "I think I love you."

43

Thomas kissed her again. His mouth hesitated on her cheek. He gently unbuttoned her blouse while his hands explored her dark brown breasts. Ida began to swoon. Then she remembered her mother. "No, Thomas," she pushed his hands away and buttoned her blouse. "Stop."

"But I love you," Thomas complained. "I love you. This is what people do when they love each other."

Passing clouds covered the sun and shadows enveloped their bodies. The wind rustled the leaves again.

"I'm not ready," Ida said, standing. She gave a penetrating look. "My Mama . . ."

"Your Mama? Your Mama ain going to be around all your life, Ida. I love you. I want you. Don't I mean anything to you?"

Yes, Thomas, but I'm not ready. I've just learned to kiss. Give me time," Ida said bitterly.

His voice dropped. "That means you don't love me." Thomas folded his arms across his chest.

"It doesn't mean that," Ida said. "You're not listening. It's about my Mama . . ."

"When are you going to grow up, Ida? You're Mama's not going to be around forever. Don't you see she's controlling your life?"

Ida nodded. "I know."

"Then?"

"Then what?"

"Then let me show you how to love."

"No," Ida said staunchly.

"I'll be waiting forever. You don't care about me. All you care about is your Mama!" Thomas stood up.

Ida sat on the bench again. She paused and looked up. "Why are you being difficult?" Ida asked.

His eyes narrowed. "Let's go to my house," Thomas said flatly. "I'm sorry. If you're afraid, I can teach you how to love. I can show you what to do. I love you and I really want you."

"I can't," Ida said cautiously. Her eyes fixed indifferently ahead.

"I'll be gentle," Thomas added more seriously.

"No," Ida said firmly.

"Then I can't wait. I can't waste my time with a girl like you," Thomas said, walking away.

He disappeared between the trees. Ida huddled in the corner of the bench, longing for him to come back, but she didn't call out for him. She felt abandoned, knowing he would never return. Ida cried, with her head bowed in her hands.

CHAPTER 10

Every summer, Beatrice, now a seventeen-year-old, would visit her grandmother's small blue and white house in Alabama. It was out in the middle of nowhere—a deserted place with dirt paths and heavy dust suspended in the air. The house, set back a few feet from the tree-lined road, was protected by faded blue shutters and an old peeling white picket fence, tangled with green vines. On a balmy evening, when the windows were open, the engines of trucks carrying coal hummed by.

Beatrice was often awakened in the middle of the night by a stream of milky moonlight that came in through the cracks of the bedroom's wooden plank walls. The eerie stillness of the country South frightened her. She begged Grandmama to take her into town where she could meet some friends, but Grandmama, too old and fragile, refused.

One evening, when Beatrice couldn't stand the stifling silence any longer, she quietly slipped out the back door into the darkness. Lighting a cigarette, Beatrice walked for a long time down a dirt path beneath the moonlight, following the North Star. Owls hooted. Crickets chirped. A gentle warm breeze blew her white and pink dress between her legs.

She finally found a cluster of homes and small buildings, with lights in the windows flickering like candles. The soft glow lit up white against the black sky. Leaning against a large tree, Beatrice bit down hard on the filter of her cigarette and forced its last smoke from her lips. She crushed the butt into the ground with her black high heels.

As Beatrice approached the glowing lights of the town, she heard a rustling in the high weeds behind her. She stopped. Then the rustling stopped. She walked a few steps more and the rustling started again. Beatrice stopped. The rustling behind her stopped once again. This time, Beatrice walked faster.

"Hey, nigger," a voice called out from behind.

"Hey, nigger," another deep voice rang out. "Don't you know we don't allow your kind around here."

Beatrice stopped and turned around. "I'm sorry," she trembled, her hands gently shaking at her sides. "I'm not from these parts here. I'm from the North. I didn't know."

"So you're one of those uppity ones. Done been up North, now she's thinkin she's white," another man said with a blind smile. "Do you know what we do to uppity niggers in these parts?"

Beatrice was suddenly drowned in a deluge of loud voices. White faces, with movements mimicking mechanical machines, gestured in slow motion. "No, please," Beatrice pleaded. "No." Her voice drooped tragically.

A hand flew up as she received the first blow. She screamed. Another hand shot up and Beatrice shrank against the stump of a tree. She felt piercing pain from the beatings about her face. Beatrice struggled to cry, but fear crowded the tears out of her eyes. It was the fear that if she made a sound, they would kill her boldly in the middle of the field. She whimpered weakly, her arms reaching out into the darkness. Thunderous thrusts burst between her legs. She felt her body spin out of control, a dark woman without power, invisible in the darkness of night. Her body grew numb as shadows suppressed her. Paralyzed, the blood flowed and dried all over her dress, leaving her body cold and shaking. Although her cries tapered to a moan, her screams persisted in the silence.

Beatrice's mother brought her home to Princeton soon after the beating and rape. They filed charges in Alabama, but Negro lawyers in New York told them it would be a lost cause. The Sheriff claimed that Beatrice couldn't identify her attackers. There would be no trial if she couldn't give an accurate description of the men.

Beatrice refused visitors for her first two weeks, but Ida and Florence caught a glimpse of her sitting on the porch one Sunday afternoon. "Beatrice," Ida waved gently from the sidewalk. "We've missed you. Are you all right?"

"I heard," Florence began softly as she climbed the stairs of the porch. "It must be so horrible. I'm happy you're back home."

Beatrice, with a pair of green-tinted sunglasses that hid her swollen eyes, sat motionless in the white rocking chair. Her battered dark face stared out at them, creating a sinister effect. Beatrice plied her husky voice in sound depths of anguish beneath a surface coolness, her upper lip curling in a twitch. She squirmed, looked away from them, and answered briefly. "It was horrible," she whispered. "I want to die." Her speech was slow and her movements stiff and labored.

Florence put their arms around Beatrice. Ida, her hands faltering, caressed the top of her rough hair. The wind blew gently in the shadows. Beatrice cried. And in between all this, she let out bit by bit, and most reluctantly, the details of her ordeal.

CHAPTER 11

There's no good time to receive bad news, but some times are worse than others. Two servants left Rosedale suddenly, leaving Carnethia with an overload of chores. Exhausted and cranky, she sat at the head of the wooden kitchen table for a small break, with her head almost resting upon its surface.

Ida, now an ebullient eighteen-year-old woman with a large smile, had something important to share with her mother. She had received notification of acceptance to Tuskegee Institute in Alabama by early April, but she kept the news secret until now. With two bags packed and placed by the front door, Ida quietly strolled through the first floor, reminiscing. Her fingertips glided over the white marble mantle in the parlor. She peered outside through the French doors. As a child, Ida remembered spending afternoons serenaded by robins on Rosedale's balconies, observing nature and gazing into the valley. She thought about last night's dinner of chicken dumplings.

Ida had spent much of her life in this house, so much time that she had worn a permanent path through the garden between two patios where she played. Suddenly, the memories were whisked away by a gust of wind as she opened the French door. Ida took a deep breath, feeling the warmth of the breeze against her face. Closing the door, she walked upstairs to the servant's kitchen to find her mother.

In the hallway's dim light, Ida heard her mother sigh from the kitchen. With hands trembling at her sides, she took another deep breath and stepped into the light of the room. Ida cleared her throat. "Mama, my teachers from school think I have a lot of potential. They have submitted my records and work and . . . " Ida started.

"And? Get to the point child," Carnethia said irritably. She gave Ida a hard glare.

"And I'm going to college, Mama. I'm leaving this afternoon for Tuskegee, Alabama to take up teaching. Everything is paid for," Ida said.

Carnethia sat up. "How do you mean?" she asked. "Leavin?"

"I'm going to college. I'm leaving this afternoon. My bags are all packed downstairs. Look," Ida said, walking out the kitchen to the staircase. Carnethia rose slowly, following behind. Ida pointed to the two bags next to the front door.

"Child, you ain't goin nowhere. Especially down South and you ain't even asked my permission. How many times have I told you it's rough down there. There's lynchin of colored folk every day. Look at what happened to Beatrice," Carnethia warned.

Ida's voice shrilled with rage. "Not again, Mama. You never listen to me."

"I always listen, but you're just a hardheaded little girl. You've always been. And what you reap, you're goin to sow one of these days." Carnethia shrugged, looking defiant.

The discussion was like the fantasy of a play viewed from a balcony.

Ida closed her eyes, pretending this was a dream. "Mama, sometimes I pretend that you understand. But you never do and you never will. I know what I'm doing. I want to teach," she protested.

"You can teach all you want up here. You ain't goin nowhere," Carnethia said, shaking her head. Her eyes moved away from Ida's face into the darkness of the hallway.

"I don't need your permission, Mama. I'm old enough. I'm all grown up now. It's my chance to do something with my life," Ida explained.

"How do you mean?" Carnethia said, placing her hands on her hips. "You an uppity thing, aren't you? You think you too good to scrub floors, don you? My dirty hands been done scrubbed years for you. What makes you think you better than me, huh?" Carnethia's hand drew close to Ida's face.

Ida glanced at her mother's wrinkled dark hands, failing to remember a time when they hugged and caressed her. Then she looked away at the floor.

"And no white family's goin to want a colored teacher anyhow," Carnethia shrugged.

"Then I'll teach my own, Mama. Colored children need to learn how to read and write too. I want a better life, Mama. I want my children to have a better life. Colored folk deserve better, Mama," Ida replied.

There was a long pause. Ida's triumphant cheery face stared at her mother's boring expression.

"How do you mean? I've done better. We live up in this nice house. You didn have to grow up with a whip at your back, picking crops under the sun, did you? I've done better," Carnethia sucked her teeth.

"Mama, I know you have worked hard, but I want more. Can't I have more?" Ida asked.

Carnethia glared hard at Ida, staring at her full breasts bulging softly beneath her white blouse. "You think you grown, don you? You ain't too big for me to put a hurtin on you. You still my daughter, no matter how big you get." Carnethia swung with an open palm against Ida's face. "There," she grinned. Her sarcastic chuckle filled the air and echoed throughout the house. Carnethia squinted at Ida. "There. Don ever sass me again, do you hear?" She swung again, using the back of her hand.

Ida had not flinched. She looked indifferently ahead. "Goodbye, Mama," she said, walking down the stairs and opening the door. "I'm going south to school. I won't be back."

Ida disappeared into the tranquil sunlight as she closed the door softly. The walls grew dark. Carnethia remained in the deep, dreary shadows of the house. The chill of desertion, helplessly watching her daughter leave Rosedale, persisted in the silence.

CHAPTER 12

Sometimes the future lies at the end of railroad tracks. Trains continued to leave New York regularly at the end of World War I, filled with orphans from the streets. Some hated the homeless children. They blamed immigrants for the scourge. Others wanted to help. The Children's Aid Society took in three little boys whose father put them out because their mother died. Another single mother could not afford to keep her daughter. Some children were dropped off in rags with only a note pinned to their chests saying, "Take care of me, please." The Children's Aid Society sent the "Orphan Trains" west for seventy thousand children who did not have homes, but no ray of light penetrated the dark gloom.

There were so many children living on the street in the squalor of tenements on the East Side. One hundred and twenty-eight children in forty families on Mulberry Street. Children in the thousands were overcrowded in schools. Young boys drank beer from milk cans in rat-infested halls on Bayard Street. The poor shivered in their homes. Children fought for warm spots from steam on street grates, near noisy underground printing press rooms when snow iced the streets in winter. Others played craps beneath the banana docks on the East River, hiding from the summer's sweltering heat.

Fifteen children crouched in a dirt alley four feet wide, with bare brick walls like a chicken coop, where the sun never rises or sets. Young ones peddled and begged. They slept on piles of straw on mud floors with only crust bread in their bellies. Babies were left by young mothers crying, helpless in the darkness of night. Tiny bodies were drowned in the East River. Croup, cholera, and Spanish influenza brought black chariots of sickness and death.

Death had no boundaries. The terrible influenza pandemic of 1919 did not spare Princeton. Many people died. A makeshift hospital was made. The following year, money was raised for a permanent hospital on the former Grover farm at the end of Witherspoon Street.

The Spanish flu also touched the Rosedale house. Miss Daisy lost her beloved mother to the illness. Barker and Miss Daisy left for Charleston to attend the funeral and burial. When they returned to Princeton, many friends and visitors came to Rosedale to express their condolences. Reverend Sykes, a man with thinning gray hair and thick spectacles, visited often. Despite his efforts, Miss Daisy remained grief-stricken and depressed, shutting herself in the darkness of her bedroom for nearly two months.

CHAPTER 13

Baseball! Baseball! Ring Lardner, an American author turned sportswriter, wrote about home runs and high-scoring games in 1920. Home run totals climbed from 138 to 261. Babe Ruth opened the decade by hitting a record fifty-four home runs—more than twice the number hit in a season. New York legalized Sunday baseball. Fans ate hot dogs. The crack of the bat on a hot summer's day made the crowds roar. Foster's National Negro Baseball League was formed. Baseball's attendance had taken off with the booming post-war economy.

Barker spent most weekends away from Rosedale and Miss Daisy, attending baseball games in New York. Some weekends he spent visiting New York office buildings and restaurants designed by architect and modernist, William Van Alen. The Standard Arcade, a two-story arcade of shops at 50 Broadway, and the Albemarle, an office building at the northwest corner of Broadway and 24th Street noted for the lack of a cornice, were among Barker's favorite buildings.

In 1924, Van Alen designed the new and spectacular Childs Restaurant, at 604 Fifth Avenue at 49th Street. The building was made with a curved corner, wrapping back to the side wall so that the building overlooked a beautiful church garden, effectively doubling the frontage. Everybody noticed. Newspaper photographers came with flashbulbs. Barker frequented the restaurant because of its fame and ambiance.

Saturday, September 20, 1924 was a clear, shining afternoon in New York, a world away from the Princeton rain. A few colored leaves hinted at autumn. Barker and Christine sat next to a window at the Childs Restaurant, overlooking the busy landscape crowded with people. A place of stark simplicity and visual elegance, the restaurant provided a quaint romantic atmosphere. Most tables were full, except for the corner tables near the kitchen. Beyond that, those seated in the balcony contended with smoke that wafted up from the bar. Classical music played softly in the background.

Christine, with head bowed, scrutinized the left-over poached fish steak in white wine with her fork. The waiter glided toward them with the last course: traditional dacquoise, with extra layers of buttercream. A clutter of water and wine glasses on the small table forced him to place the dessert plates on the edge of the table. In slow motion, one plate tipped and Barker caught it with one hand.

"Sir, I'm so sorry," the waiter apologized.

Christine smiled. Barker nodded. "It's quite all right. I was able to catch it."

The two shared dessert quietly until Christine took the last bite. Then she abruptly asked questions about life at Rosedale. Barker proudly answered. "It has been a wonderful investment, like a beautiful museum of sorts," he started. "It's a little large. You can get lost in it easily, but it has served me as a wonderful home."

"I want to thank you for inviting me to restaurants and the theater over the years while Angus is away," Christine said, leaning on one elbow. "He's always traveling to Oxford. He has so many lectures to give there. I can't fathom what I'd do without you."

Barker grasped her hand, smiling. "It's been a pleasure. I don't know what I'd do without you either." He paused, looking deep into her eyes. "I made another reservation this afternoon. I hope you won't mind."

"Where?" Christine asked excitedly. "I thought we were going back to Princeton now."

"Are you in a hurry? Is Angus coming home?" Barker asked nervously.

"No, he doesn't come home until next week," Christine answered. "What reservation do you have?"

"I thought it was time to spend an evening at a hotel," Barker said, looking down at the table.

"Do you mean overnight?" Christine asked.

Barker nodded. "I've ordered room service, a dinner with champagne. I'd love to have your company."

Christine was wary at first, but she was also lonely and complacent enough to let down her guard. "I don't know, Barker. I'd like to, but I don't know if we should. What happens if Daisy finds out or Angus finds out or . . ."

Barker placed his fingertip on Christine's red lips, silencing her. He leaned over and poured his mouth into hers. Christine gazed into his eyes.

"Angus is away. Daisy is in Princeton. We know how we feel about each other. I love your attention. I love your letters. I want you, Christine. I know you want me."

Christine looked away.

"Will you come?" Barker persisted, tugging gently at her arm. "I don't want to be disappointed."

He stood, grabbing her hand. Christine quietly followed through the restaurant's swirling smoke like a gray mist, out the front door beneath the shadows of skyscrapers.

Miss Daisy, engaged in the simple rhythm of her days, decided to clean closets and rearrange furniture in the master bedroom. Four servants moved bookcases and chairs. There was screeching and grinding across the wooden floor. Miss Daisy sat on the edge of her bed, sorting through Barker's suits.

"Carnethia, we need to put some of these aside for charity. I don't believe Barker uses most of these suits anymore," Miss Daisy said, looking through suit pockets.

"Yes, ma'am," Carnethia smiled, taking a suit from Miss Daisy.

She removed his gold pocket watch from another suit and showed it to Carnethia. "Now you see, if I didn't check his pockets, this expensive watch would go to charity too." She shook her head from side to side, feeling through inner pockets. "Now there's more in this suit," Miss Daisy chuckled, removing a folded paper and two theater ticket stubs. "What are these?" She hesitated. "Barker and I haven't been to the theater in months." She glanced at the ticket dates from two weeks ago. Miss Daisy, a little frantic, stood and paced the floor. "Barker never told me he went to the theater two weeks ago. I think he said he went to a baseball game."

"I don't know, ma'am," Carnethia said, looking over her shoulder.

Miss Daisy unfolded the paper and began to read. There was a long pause. Her distress spread like a bad fog.

"What's the matter, Miss Daisy," Carnethia asked.

"Oh, my, it's what I've thought and dreaded all these years," Miss Daisy said. "Christine. It's a love letter from Christine, Professor Angus's wife. They've been seeing each other." The letter fell to the floor.

In rage, Miss Daisy grabbed the gold pocket watch and slammed it against the wall. Time stopped. Broken glass sprayed to the floor. Startled, the servants left the room, all except Carnethia. "Miss Daisy," Carnethia whispered, picking up glass with her fingertips. "Miss Daisy, please sit down."

"Sit down? Sit down? I have spent my entire life and fortune with Barker here at Rosedale and he decides to spend time with Christine? We left everything in Charleston to come here. After building Rosedale, this house beckoned me, like Barker beckoned me for marriage. I thought it was meant for me to take care of this house and Barker for the rest of my life. It all felt perfect. This was supposed to be perfect. This was supposed to be forever. Am I so misled?" Miss Daisy looked confused. "I don't understand. Am I not beautiful enough? Aren't my manners fine enough? Christine can offer nothing to Barker. I wonder if Professor Angus knows anything about this. I'll be sure to show him this note."

"Calm down, Miss Daisy," Carnethia said, placing her arm around her shoulder. "I don want nothin to happen to you."

"Nothing will happen to me. Something will happen to Christine and Barker. Barker isn't due home until tomorrow evening. I will confront him then. I just don't believe this. I just don't believe this," Miss Daisy cried.

Carnethia served Miss Daisy a cup of tea. "There, there, Miss Daisy. Maybe it all ain't true. It will be all right."

"No," Miss Daisy sipped tea. "No, it's not all right. I'll be waiting for Barker when he comes home tomorrow evening. I'll be waiting," Miss Daisy promised.

A shadow of fearful anticipation enveloped Rosedale. Miss Daisy, with eyes grieved and bitter in a long black dress, sat quietly in the darkness of the parlor Sunday evening, waiting. The caretakers and servants were sent away for the evening. Finally, a sudden gust of wind like a loud sigh passed through the house. It gently shook the chandelier and rustled the draperies. A shadow of fearful anticipation enveloped the house. Miss Daisy called from the parlor. "Barker? Barker, is that you?"

"Daisy," Barker said, scurrying inside from the pelting rain. "It's lousy weather out there. New York was so sunny. It's funny how the weather can be so different only a few hours away. Where are you? Why are you in the dark down here?" He turned on a light in the foyer.

"I'm here in the parlor," Miss Daisy said softly, clutching the folded letter in her hands.

His voice was light, almost happy as he lit a cigar. "Then turn on the light," Barker said, coming closer.

Miss Daisy turned on a small, dim lamp. The light cast shadows about her face.

"I've missed you," Barker said, kissing her cheek.

Miss Daisy withdrew. "Don't bother, Barker. Don't kiss me."

"You're acting awfully strange. Are you all right? Are you feeling ill?" His eyes darted quickly around the room. "What's that in your hand?"

"I hate you," Miss Daisy said, giving him a sharp look. "I hate you." She turned, frowning.

"What are you talking about?" Barker asked, stepping toward Miss Daisy. He was standing over her now, his strong, masculine shadow blocking the light from the lamp. "What's wrong?"

Miss Daisy struck, pummeling his chest with her fists. Books from the nearby shelf crashed to the floor. It was an occasion of profound alarm for Barker. Miss Daisy's insults flung in the heat of rage. He grabbed her wrists to restrain her. "Daisy, you've gone mad," Barker warned.

Miss Daisy shouted in a shrill of anger. "I found your theater tickets. I found your love letter. It's been Christine all along, hasn't it? You tell me you're going to the baseball game with clients. You spend weekends in New York. You were with her, weren't you?"

Barker wet his lips and said nothing.

"Answer me, Barker," Miss Daisy demanded.

Barker tried to avoid her eyes, but he could not hide. "Daisy, all you've cared about since we've built Rosedale is this house and getting into Miss Katherine's club at the university. You haven't paid me any attention. You have more of a relationship with this house than me. You don't love me. You're more in love with this house."

"That's a lie! I've done everything for you. This house is about you! Don't give me any excuses," Miss Daisy cried.

"I don't love you, Daisy. I haven't loved you for a long time. I want a divorce." Barker turned away.

"To marry Christine? What about Angus?" Miss Daisy screamed.

"Christine won't marry me. Believe me, I've asked her. I want a divorce anyway. There's nothing left for me here, just you and this house," he complained.

Her voice drooped tragically. "How could you do this? How could you?" Miss Daisy pleaded. She raised her eyes to Barker, with tears exhausted in her pale drawn face.

"I'll be spending the night elsewhere," Barker said, reaching for his coat. "Good night."

The door slammed shut. The dark silence was dreary and oppressive. Rain beat down hard upon Rosedale. Huddled in the parlor chair, Miss Daisy cried herself to sleep.

CHAPTER 14

The misty, magical Sourland Mountains, a ten-mile ridge of hardwood trees rising from the Delaware River near Lambertville in west central New Jersey, spans northeast to Woods Tavern through three counties and four townships. Standing 568 feet at its highest point, it is surrounded by dense woods filled with boulders, rolling farmland, and narrow winding roads that snaked like mountain switchbacks.

The Lenape were its first inhabitants. George Washington gathered Henry Knox, the Marquis de Lafayette, Baron Friedrich Wilhelm von Steuben, Nathanael Greene, Anthony Wayne, and "Light-Horse Harry" Lee for strategic sessions in the Hunt House on Province Line Road before the Battle of Monmouth. Harry "Put," a former slave of General Rufus Putnam, made charcoal from the mountain. Some brewed moonshine during Prohibition, hiding away behind these dense forest facades.

In 1932, the Lindbergh baby, Charles A. Jr., was kidnapped from Highfields on Hopewell-Wertsville Road. On Sundays, cars parked for blocks to get a glimpse of Lindbergh. Pilots charged a dollar to fly visitors over the house. Mountain folk sent reporters on goose chases down the worst dirt roads.

The subsequent trial of Bruno Hauptmann in nearby Flemington was not the only excitement in the country. Franklin D. Roosevelt gave a dinner to Booker T. Washington in the White House. A momentous change came over the United States when Roosevelt established new jobs after the Depression, giving jobs to those out of work.

New Jersey created one hundred thousand jobs. The Civilian Conservation Corps hired men to work on conservation projects. Men built wildlife shelters. They stocked streams with fish and planted trees. Others got work putting in sewers. Some built schools, highways, and bridges. Even a new boardwalk in Cape May was constructed.

Ida and her husband, with two young children, moved back to Princeton for work, finding a small house for rent on John Street. Her eyes were filled with emotion when she returned. She had not seen her mother in fourteen years. Florence and Beatrice had long stopped writing. It would take some time to meet new neighbors and friends. There was a new house to furnish and small children to take care of. Soon she found a job as a teacher at the John Witherspoon Street School for the Colored.

CHAPTER 15

Arthur Bennett, a brown-skinned seven-year-old with rough black hair parted on the side, hunched over his desk crammed with loose papers and books, the edges sticking out on all sides. He was making a story book. He began with two main characters, a dog and a cat, dancing on a porch.

Arthur drew the animals simply. The dog was black with a red tongue and thick tail. The cat was brown with one white eye. He worked quickly, humming and fidgeting, barely able to contain his excitement. As Arthur drew, he whispered words about the story. "They're dancin because they're happy. It's Sunday, so they can have some fun," he said without looking up from his crayons.

Ida stood above him. Arthur looked up. "That's good, Arthur," she said, touching his shoulder. "Just try to work quieter, please."

"You like it," Miss Ida B.?" Arthur grinned.

"Yes, I do," Ida said, nodding.

Ida taught fourteen first and second graders at the Witherspoon Street School for the Colored. This afternoon, they worked at their desks in a small cluttered classroom, like a shoe box, stuffed with students, second-hand books, maps, and globes from the white Nassau Street school. Ida sat in a corner with a group of five beginning readers. She used white cards to help them put sounds together into syllables. Then she asked a student to read from a small book.

Mary Ann, a slight dark-skinned girl with glasses, stood before the group sitting in a semi-circle. She read slowly, with a clear and varied tone. Mary Ann paused, shifting from side to side, then fiddled with her black braids. She spoke and paused again while two girls giggled. Her hands, holding the book, shook slightly. After reading three sentences, the children applauded.

"Very nice, Mary Ann," Ida smiled. "You must be practicing your reading at home."

"I am, Miss Ida B. My Mama practice reading every night with me. My Mama says that's the only way I can go to college one day," Mary Ann said, ending her sentence with a giggle. The girl pulled a book from her bag, hanging from the back of her carved-up and scratched wooden chair. She opened the book to the first page. "I can read this book too."

Suddenly, a small light-skinned child ran to the back row of the classroom over crumpled papers left on the floor. He threw his body face down over the desk and sobbed.

"Oh my," Ida said softly, touching his shoulder. "What happened?"

The little boy, with his face hidden, continued to cry.

"Shhh, Michael," Ida comforted. "We can talk about this. Let me dismiss the class first. It's time to go home anyway." Ida looked up and snapped her fingers. "Class, it's time to go home. Remember the homework. I'll see you tomorrow."

Michael sat up quietly, wiping the tears from his eyes as his classmates noisily ran around gathering their books and coats. He wrapped his feet around the legs of his chair and fidgeted with a red crayon.

When the classroom was quiet, Ida sat next to Michael. "So what happened?" Ida asked.

Michael, an eight-year-old, was a combination of shyness and arrogance. His speech was interrupted by ums and ahs as he stuttered searching for the right words. "Miss Ida B., when I went to the bathroom, there were kids making fun of me," he started.

"What did they say?" Ida asked, arching her eyebrows.

"They say I'm stupid. They say I can't talk. They say my skin is white and I don't belong here." Michael began to cry again.

"There, there," Ida rubbed his shoulder. "Some children say such cruel things."

"But they say them every day. I hate this school!" Michael cried.

"Michael, you are a beautiful little boy. Now don't let any one of these children stop you from being beautiful, do you hear me? Not everyone will be happy with who you are, but you must be happy with who you are. Be proud of yourself, Michael. Be proud to be you. You're making such fine progress in class. Don't let them stop you from being the beautiful child that you are." Ida hugged Michael as she walked him to the door.

Michael disappeared as he walked beneath maple trees from the school down the steps to the street. Ida waved goodbye. She tried to maintain a strong optimism for her students, but sometimes there seemed to be so much against them. "Be strong, my child," she said in a prayerful whisper. "Be strong, it's just the beginning." She shook her head from side to side. Then she stopped to watch a blue jay perched on the branch, noting its beauty. The sun illuminated her face before sinking over the valley.

It was a black, moonless evening. The front porch and living room were dark when Ida arrived home. She unlocked the front door and struggled to feel for the light switch. When the light was turned on, it was as if the living room were an oyster opened up to reveal a luminous pearl. The green living room was cluttered, but comfortable. An old grand piano stood in the corner with bookshelves leaning on each side. Several small and large paintings were scattered on the walls. The black coffee table, scarred with cigarette burns and filled with old photographs, was in the center in front of an old sofa.

"Is that you, Ida?" a voice bellowed from upstairs. "Com on up. You have a surprise waiting for you."

"It's me," Ida chirped. "John, what kind of surprise?"

John, a brown-skinned man with coarse hair brushed flat, was sitting at the top of the stairs with their four-year-old daughter Betty on his lap. She was wearing a green dress and two white barrettes in her hair. "Hi, Mommy," she waved excitedly.

"Hi, baby," Ida greeted her.

"The surprise is up in Timmy's bedroom," John said.

The baby, Timmy, suddenly cried in a feverish pitch. "I know the baby hasn't been put to sleep yet," Ida said with her hands on her hips. "He's crying too loud for that." She squeezed past her husband and child on the stairs and walked into the bedroom.

A tall faded brown woman, no longer young, stood holding Timmy in her arms. She was clothed in a green flowered dress that fell straight, hiding the thinness of her bones. Her lean shadow cut through the lamp's light. Timmy, with thick black hair and puffy cheeks and wearing a blue nightgown, arched his back a bit and whimpered. He was just slightly smaller than the average six month old. His brown skin was well oiled and healthy.

For a few moments, the two women looked at each other in silence.

"Mama?" Ida hesitated. "Mama, is that you?"

"Yes, Ida. I have some beautiful grandchildren. And your husband, what a nice choice of a man," Carnethia's voice quivered. "I'm so sorry it's taken me this long to meet them. I've missed so much."

As she spoke, Ida watched the shifting patterns of light on her mother's face. Ida's eyes darted away. "I can't believe you are here. You never once visited me in the South. You missed my graduation. You missed our wedding. You missed my birthing these children," Ida said angrily.

Timmy's dark brown eyes darted around the room, following the sound of voices.

"He's quite an active baby. He likes to look around," Carnethia smiled.

"Mama, answer me," Ida demanded.

"I'm here now," Carnethia said uneasy. "I'm here now. Please forgive me, child. I was angry. I didn't want you to leave me. I didn't want you to grow up. I wanted you to stay safe home with me. I needed you here with me, but you were so stubborn, so hard-headed, so independent. I was afraid for you in the South with all that lynchin down there. I was hopin you'd miss me and com on home to me, baby. That's why I never came. Please forgive me." She wiped tears from her dark brown eyes.

"Come here, let me see you," Carnethia said, placing the baby in the crib.

Ida took two steps forward and turned on the ceiling light. Beneath the bedroom light, Ida's face glistened. Carnethia grabbed her arm, remembering. "Look at you, all filled out and all," she said, looking at the pearls around Ida's neck that gently touched her large bosom. "You're not a child anymore. I almost don recognize you. You turned out to be such a beautiful woman." Carnethia stared with such awe and respect. Then she kissed Ida's cheek.

Ida drew back in aversion. Slowly, she lowered her face. "Mama, I'm glad to see you too, but it's been so long. You just didn't care. You always wrote that you couldn't come to see me. Miss Daisy, Miss Daisy. Your excuse was always tending to Miss Daisy. She'd give you time off if you asked. She'd give you time off for my graduation and my wedding. I'm tired of you can't," Ida said, folding her arms across her chest.

Carnethia paused and looked. "This will take some time," her voice dropped.

Ida nodded, understanding.

"Blamin you or blamin me won't get us nowhere," Carnethia said sadly. "I know I've got a lot to make up to you."

Ida hesitated for a moment, then added quietly. "Mama, I just need some time."

"May I come to visit again?" Carnethia asked. "Maybe next Sunday afternoon?"

"Yes, Mama," Ida said bitterly. "Why don't you plan to stay for supper with us too."

"I'd like that," Carnethia said. "Thank you. Please forgive me, child. I'm so sorry. Please forgive me." Carnethia left the room and the house, into the darkness of the starless night.

CHAPTER 16

Albert Einstein, a fifty-four-year-old refugee from Nazi Germany, arrived in Princeton with his second wife, Elsa, on October 17, 1933. By the time he came to live in the United States, he had already developed astounding scientific theories about time, space, gravity, matter, and the universe.

He had visited Princeton earlier in 1921 when Princeton University awarded him an honorary degree, but the decision to reside permanently in Princeton came about through the persuasion of Abraham Flexner, an educator. He wanted Einstein to be the first member of the community devoted to scholarship at the Institute of Advanced Studies.

Horrific events in Germany also helped to change Einstein's mind. Germany was no longer safe for Jews. Nazis burned his books. The street in Ulm, Germany dedicated in honor of Einstein in the early 1920s called Einsteinstrasse was changed in the early 1930s. The Nazis could not bear to see a Jew like Einstein honored, whose lifestyle, work, and mind symbolized all that they wanted to destroy.

When Hitler came to power, Einstein announced his decision to live in Princeton and soon moved into a small two-story Colonial house with a porch and black shutters on Mercer Street.

Einstein's arrival as a permanent faculty member at the Institute of Advanced Studies gave the institution its identity. Everyone talked around Einstein, watching and listening closely. He gave lectures. The music of Beethoven played. Other distinguished professors from the United States and Europe were attracted to Einstein's presence in Princeton.

Although Einstein was well respected by fellow faculty and students and found sanctuary in Princeton from the troubles of Europe, Einstein described his new home to Queen Elizabeth of Belgium in a letter this way: "Princeton is a wonderful little spot, a quaint and ceremonious village of puny demigods on stilts. . . . Here the people who compose what is called 'society' enjoy even less freedom than their counterparts in Europe. Yet they seem unaware of this restriction, since their way of life tends to inhibit personality development from childhood."

Despite his feelings, Einstein became acquainted with his new home. He walked and shopped along the streets of Princeton. Nassau Street was filled with the clanging of trolleys, the clatter of horse and buggies, and the horns of automobiles. Street workers fanned themselves with their caps. Italian men trimmed gardens and lawns. Boys in knickers ran along the sides of cars carrying bundles for delivery. The washwomen came up from Witherspoon Street and the trolley lines, crossing Nassau Street to work at the University.

Einstein was a great scientist with elaborate ideas to the exclusion of everyone else. Brilliant and unsophisticated, some Princetonians found Einstein to be eccentric. Soon Einstein became a source of community gossip, but he seemed to enjoy life. He sailed on Lake Carnegie, talked with neighborhood children, played the violin, wrote poetry, and ate ice cream.

Ida first encountered Dr. Einstein as she stood in line behind him, his head full of white bushy hair wrapped in a muffler. He bought flowers in a shop on Nassau Street. It seems he never bought flowers by the dozen, but always in odd numbers, which often stumped the clerks waiting on him and caused giggles from customers inside the store.

A few years later, Ida saw Einstein again in the early morning hours on the Princeton Railroad platform as she waited for the train to Trenton. A porter pushed his large broom across the platform between them. Ida knew this to be the famous man that everyone in town gossiped about and dreamed of meeting him one day, but it was impolite for colored folk to make their acquaintance with such an important man.

She watched him out of the corner of her eye, pacing between wooden posts, with his long shaggy gray hair, a gray cashmere sweater, baggy unpressed trousers, and sockless feet. He started from one end of the platform, making a right turn between two posts, then a left turn around another post, and made an about-face. He did this repeatedly until the train came.

Once he caught a glimpse of Ida watching him. She quickly adverted her eyes toward the ground and looked up. He stopped pacing for a few seconds and smiled at her. She nervously smiled back and nodded graciously, looking at his deep set eyes. For a moment, they seemed to understand each other.

A despair seized Ida when Einstein disappeared into the front of the shuttle and she stepped aboard the rear. Ida sat in a window seat. The train began to move slowly along steel stripes, the crisscrossing metal designed to bring civilization closer together. It picked up speed, blurring the town of Princeton behind. The wind came up suddenly, rustling the autumn leaves, turning the sky overcast almost dark as slate.

CHAPTER 17

By the winter of 1934, Daisy Gummere was a pitiful figure of suffering. At the age of forty-nine, Miss Daisy's face looked pale and tired. Her long disheveled hair was now streaked gray. She no longer possessed the grace of a determined woman imbued with confidence. Most days, she lay sprawled amid rumpled sheets in bed, with the curtains drawn. She gazed at Barker's broken pocket watch on the end table, its time frozen a little after nine, the time when she learned of his affair with Christine. Miss Daisy held the dusty white ribbon saved from her wedding bouquet between her wrinkled fingers, remembering. A bottle of gin was hidden in her top bureau drawer, and she regularly took swigs that stung her mouth, tracing a line down her throat, illuminating her insides.

Miss Daisy had hemorrhoids and migraine headaches. She had endured Barker's infidelities and the insularism of Princeton University's women. Carnethia, her most beloved and dependable servant, had passed away. Her servants and caretakers diminished to only a few. But there was something distinctly different about her aches and pains now; in a neurotic way, it was unleashing a different spirit.

"I don't eat or sleep. Sometimes it's hard to stay awake. I dread waking up to the world. Barker is rarely home. Visitors don't stop by. And no matter what I do, I'm not accepted. I'm alone in a world full of beautiful things. Alone with my beautiful paradise of misery and nothing. It's nearly impossible to endure life anymore. So I ask, why am I here? What am I to do? What am I to do?" Miss Daisy wrote in her white diary decorated with red and pink roses.

"Miss Daisy." A servant opened the bedroom door. Unfettered sunlight filled the bedroom. "You have a visitor. It's just Reverend Sykes."

"My, my." Miss Daisy tried to fix her hair with her fingers. "Let me get a robe on. Send him up in a few minutes." She put on the tiny gold cross sparkling in a stream of sunlight on the bureau. It glinted in the neckline of her simple white robe.

"Miss Daisy," a voice echoed behind the door. "May I come in?"

"Why, yes," Miss Daisy said, opening the bedroom draperies. "It's nice of you to pay me a visit again. I must say you're about the only person who hasn't given up on me."

The morning sunlight seeped through the bedroom across the Reverend's pale face. "We're always thinking of you, Miss Daisy. There's many who send their regards. We're always praying for you. Times get hard for all of us. Everyone needs someone," he said with a grin. "Trust me." He hustled to the corner of the bedroom with a large leather bag, its strap slung over his scrawny shoulder, spilling over with Bibles and papers. Still talking, he pulled a Bible from the bag and sat down.

"It's hard to trust anymore," Miss Daisy said sadly, leaning forward with one elbow in her knee. "Life is miserable. My marriage was supposed to last forever. What's trust these days?" She gently touched the white wedding ribbon on the end table.

Reverend Sykes opened his black Bible and read from Revelation 21:4, trying to celebrate a hope and ease the distress that Miss Daisy said would never go away.

"He will wipe every tear from their eyes. Death will be no more, neither mourning nor outcry nor pain will be anymore. The former things have passed away," Reverend Sykes read softly.

"If not passed away, things have certainly changed," Miss Daisy said, frowning at her hands, then settled into a thought. "I've lost my husband to other women. It's like death. And I'm reminded of it often. Sometimes I think I hear his laughter in the emptiness and darkness of this house. His old pocket watch has stopped ticking. It will stay that way forever." She paused, looking around the bedroom. "And someone must clean out his clothes from the closets. Someone must teach me how to take over the house and few investments I have left." Miss Daisy held a wedding photograph, trimmed in silver, in both hands. The photograph, with Barker and Miss Daisy arm in arm, was yet unmarked by distressful events, the faces of two young lovers who, before this, were two people smiling for the camera on the happiest day of their lives.

"Trust me," Reverend Sykes extended his hand. Miss Daisy grasped his warm fingertips. "Trust me. There will be people to help you. You are never alone." He urged Miss

Daisy to have faith, even as she tried to understand how this could have happened.

She shook her head from side to side. "It's quite difficult. I never imagined a divorce. It's so humiliating." Miss Daisy hung her head, with her hands covering her face, and sobbed. "No more house parties. No more theaters. No more splendid vacations. Without Barker, I just have such a beautiful empty house."

"God hasn't left you. He wants us to be a light of hope and love that the world needs so badly. You must get out more, Miss Daisy. It's not good for you to stay locked in the room in the darkness," he said. "We want to see your beautiful smile again. You will heal in time."

The sun gleamed brightly against the bedroom's white walls. A calm wind blew through the room. Miss Daisy nodded. "I'm trying," she said. "I'm willing to try." Her grimace turned into a slight smile, but Miss Daisy would never look at a white ribbon, even in a young girl's hair, in the same way again.

CHAPTER 18

Paul Robeson, lawyer, scholar, athlete, actor, and singer, returned to Princeton, the town that both birthed and devastated him, in 1935, to perform in his only New Jersey appearance that year at McCarter Theater.

Born in a small dingy house in Princeton's colored section in 1898, Robeson bitterly complained that Princeton was "like a southern plantation." Princeton, a town of southern aristocrats, made it tough on his family, according to Robeson. His brothers were not allowed to go to the local high school. They were sent ten miles away to attend school in Trenton. His eldest brother was distressed about the university, filled with generations of wealthy southerners who were notorious for discrimination and the policy not to accept Negro students. Negroes were told outright they were not wanted.

Almost every Negro in town lived off the college in some way and accepted the status that went with it. Robeson said for all intents and purposes, colored folk lived on a Southern plantation. And with no more dignity than it suggested—all the bowing and scraping to the drunken rich, all the vile and despicable names, all the Uncle Tomming to earn a less than modest living and a miserable life.

Despite these hardships, Paul Robeson left Princeton and went on to win letters at Rutgers in football, baseball, basketball, track, a Phi Beta Kappa key, a ninety percent scholastic average, a law degree from Columbia University, and a fine reputation for "being the perfect type of college man." With his singing fame, Robeson performed before packed houses in many large cities throughout the United States and Europe.

Paul Robeson attributed his success and determination to his father, a "self-made man" who escaped slavery on a North Carolina plantation at the age of fifteen. His father didn't have any respect for someone who didn't accomplish what he had set out to do. Like his father, Robeson believed when someone fell, a small guardian angel pulled the person up. No one could be defeated by another, not even a colored man. A person could only be defeated by themselves.

With these thoughts in mind, Robeson returned to Princeton and thrilled the audience with a magnificent concert that would benefit the Princeton YMCA. He walked about the stage, with a radiant ambiance, tapping his foot to the music's sweet rhythm and sang "Didn't It Rain" and "Nobody Knows de Trouble I've Seen." His stance, bold and erect, showed his determination. The deep richness and triumphant notes of his voice, with his irresistible personality, took hold of the audience. Everyone exploded into a standing ovation.

Miss Daisy, sitting in the front row, applauded fervently. Ida cried and clapped emotionally. She stood proudly in the back with other coloreds.

CHAPTER 19

The official opening of Palmer Square took place on September 9, 1937, with the public cordially invited. The idea, conceived by Edgar Palmer, a Princeton University graduate, and designed by architect Thomas Stapleton, turned an area of unpainted houses, barns, and rutted streets into a downtown center in the style of an eighteenth century colonial village. The "Square," as residents called it, boasted of seventy-eight magnificent stores: a new Nassau Inn, post office, and residences. The Silver Shop, Clayton's Dry Goods, and Cousin's Wines were among the first stores to open. The Princeton Playhouse, built several months later, lured townsfolk with a black and white newsreel, a comedy, then the main picture. Residents flocked to see Charlie Chaplin and Douglas Fairbanks.

But the building of the Square was not without growing pains. Some older folk opposed the creation of a larger downtown center. Others were skeptical and dismissed the idea. Nonetheless, Palmer pursued construction.

To make way for the Square, numerous buildings were demolished in a twelve-square block area fronting Nassau Street. The original two-hundred-year-old Nassau Inn, in a state of disrepair, was torn down and rebuilt. The only original piece of the inn, an old stone bench upon which wine was stored, was moved across the Square.

Old timers, sitting on benches in the Square, fondly recalled the old Nassau Inn, hosting visitors on stagecoach pit stops between Philadelphia and New York. A second-floor balcony used to serve as a reviewing stand for parades and a platform for political candidates like Roosevelt.

The neighborhood behind the original Inn, home to those who worked in Princeton's mansions and university kitchens, was gone. Baker Street disappeared. Beatrice's house was leveled. Residents were displaced. More housing was promised and built on Birch Street, atop the city dump.

Ida, walking pass the post office, reminisced about her childhood, playing with Florence on Baker Street. The autumn wind blew leaves gently across her path. Black squirrels scampered between large oak trees. Sighing, Ida imagined Beatrice's old house, their family rocking on the porch on a late Sunday afternoon. Now it was only a memory.

CHAPTER 20

Dim light filtered through the parlor, casting deep shadows across Miss Daisy's face. She cuddled next to the radio a little after eight on Halloween Eve in 1938 and fiddled with the radio dial looking for her favorite show with Edgar Bergen and his wooden-headed dummy, Charlie McCarthy. Miss Daisy came across Tchaikovsky's Piano Concerto No.1 in B-Flat Minor, the theme of the *Mercury Theater on the Air* by the Columbia Broadcasting System. She sat back in her chair and listened for a moment, swaying her head from side to side with the music.

Then a commanding voice took over the air waves. " . . . minds that are to our minds as ours are to the beasts of the jungle, intellects vast, cool, and unsympathetic, regarding this earth with envious eyes and . . ."

Miss Daisy shuddered. She immediately called for the servants to gather and listen with her in the parlor. For the next hour, they and several million people across the country were bombarded by a series of news bulletins and dance band "remotes" that began with a deliberate calm and escalated into fear and mass hysteria.

An announcer broke in with a bulletin from the "Intercontinental Radio News." He reported several explosions of incandescent gas occurring on the surface of Mars. Dance music resumed. Another news bulletin came from reporter Carl Phillips at nearby Princeton Observatory, who was conducting an interview with Professor Pierson. The professor described Mars, a red disk swimming in a blue sea, but could not give valid explanation for the explosions. Another wire from the "Natural History Museum" in New York registered a shock of earthquake intensity within a radius of twenty miles of Princeton.

Again the program returned to music, followed by more bulletins. A special announcement from Trenton: a huge, flaming object believed to be a meteorite fell on a farm in Grovers Mill, just four miles east of Princeton. The flash in the sky was visible for several hundred miles. Miss Daisy and her servants rushed to the parlor windows. They hurried to look at the sky from the front door. Seeing nothing but darkness, they returned to the parlor. One servant stared and gulped. Another servant wept bitterly. Miss Daisy clutched the small cross around her neck. Leaning closer to the radio, they listened again.

The broadcast returned to dance melodies. And again the music was interrupted by another news flash. Reporter Carl Phillips, accompanied by Professor Pierson, state troopers, and onlookers were gathering around what appeared to be a large metallic cylinder. Phillips reported hundreds of cars and headlights throwing a bright spot on the object. Some bystanders dared to get closer.

Suddenly, someone or something emerged from the object Something wriggling out of the shadows like a gray snake. It was large as a bear. It glistened. The eyes were black. Saliva dripped from its rimless lips. Thirty state troopers circled around. Then they heard a high-pitch whine of machinery. A jet flame springing from a mirror struck. Everything turned into flames. Some screamed. Other shrieked. Forty people were reported dead at Grovers Mill, their bodies burned and distorted beyond recognition. Then there was abrupt silence.

The servants didn't move. Blood drained from Miss Daisy's face. She gave the frantic command to draw every drape and curtain. They barricaded each door with chairs and heavy furniture. Rosedale gasped quietly. All lights grew dark except the small dim lamp next to the radio in the parlor. Their shadows hovered once again near the radio.

The announcer reported aliens out of control, destroying railroad tracks and communication lines from New York to Philadelphia. Highways to the north and south clogged with human traffic. Police and army reserves were deployed immediately.

A current of fear flowed throughout the country. There were phone calls to local police stations. Some called the electric company to turn off city lights to make it easier to hide in the darkness. Others drove down their streets, blasting horns as a warning. Several marched down to the police station and demanded to be evacuated. Doctors and nurses volunteered at local hospitals. College students lined up at the telephones to speak with their parents for the last time. People gathered on rooftops to watch New York City burn. Families packed cars and began to flee.

The program of doom played out the drama down to the end. There seemed little hope for humanity. Miss Daisy and her servants held hands. They prayed and sang gospel songs. They begged God to spare their lives.

Miss Daisy and her servants woke up the next morning huddled together on the parlor floor. They gave thanks to God for allowing them to live another day. Miss Daisy tuned in to a radio broadcast again. Listening carefully, she discovered the events of last night to be a hoax. It was just Orson Welles's dramatization of *War of the Worlds*.

Miss Daisy tried to regain composure, her breathing returned to normal. Everyone rejoiced. Servants carefully removed furniture from the doors. They opened draperies, letting in warm light. Miss Daisy's long gray hair glared like the sun as she peered through a window. Fallen leaves covered with frost glistened. Birds glided gently in the wind. A passing breeze through the house breathed like a sigh, but the fear and terror brought upon Rosedale on the eve of Halloween would be an event no one would forget.

CHAPTER 21

On a gray winter day in 1945, there was nothing like lunch at Griggs' Corner Restaurant on Witherspoon Street to lift your spirits. It was the hooted laughter, melodious voices, and the aroma of the best coffee around that beckoned customers, colored and white, through its doors.

The blues filtered the air, playing from a small radio at the front counter. The owner, Bennett Griggs, a lean man with a flared nose, thin lips, and burnished brown skin sweating like high gloss, hummed along as he wiped down the greasy counter. Coffee, sandwiches, barbecue and hot sauce, and chitterlings on platters were served by bustling waitresses.

Miss Daisy sat in the back of the restaurant at a red checkered table with Reverend Sykes, two colored men, and a white woman. They ordered a light lunch. Between bites of sandwiches and sipped cola, they chuckled. Miss Daisy finished eating before everyone. She smiled attentively at Reverend Sykes, rubbing her fingertips against her coffee cup. Life seemed purposeful again. She was healthier, getting out more for various volunteer efforts and social activities during the last three years. Everyone at this table worked secretly for the civil rights of colored people.

One of their activities was to "front" for colored families wanting to buy houses in white areas in the state. An attempt to move a colored family into a white neighborhood in Teaneck, New Jersey was successful. Miss Daisy and Reverend Sykes were to hold fort in the new house with the colored family for the first night.

"It's delightful that the Smith family closed on their house last week," Reverend Sykes said cheerfully.

"I'm just afraid the neighbors aren't so happy," the woman whispered. "With the writing, 'Go home, niggers' on the property last week, I'm afraid people haven't given up on getting them out."

"But it's their house now," Miss Daisy insisted. "They bought it and paid for it."

"That doesn't mean they'll be welcomed," one colored man said. "There's all sorts of things they can do to move 'em out."

The other man nodded, squinting. "That's why we need someone to stay with them for the first few nights," he thundered angrily. "We can't be victorious until families stay put in their new homes."

"We don't want them run out of town," Reverend Sykes said. "It's important that they see this is a unified effort between coloreds and whites. I'm glad we'll be able to help."

Miss Daisy smiled. "Me too. My bags are packed. We'll be leaving in two hours," she added.

Reverend Sykes gave a penetrating look. "It's important that the neighbors see our presence there. Hopefully, the writing on the walls last week was just a prank and nothing will happen," he said, leaning on the table with his elbow.

"Call us if there are problems," the woman said cautiously. "Call us a few times that evening just to let us know how you are."

The sun was still high in the blue sky when Reverend Sykes and Miss Daisy drove to Teaneck. They approached a small gray cape cod with white shutters and a freshly painted white picket fence. A large sycamore tree hung its branches over the sidewalk. Neighbors standing and talking outside stared as they strolled up the walkway to the front door. Reverend Sykes knocked. A burly dark man with a broad face and full lips greeted them. "Good afternoon," he smiled. "Reverend Sykes and Miss Daisy, how good to see you. Come in."

The white living room, overstuffed with chairs, bookcases, and boxes, looked like a crammed warehouse. The walls and windows were bare. A single embroidered rug lay on the wooden dining room floor. "We got a lot of work to do here," he said. "But it sure feels good to have your own home."

"Miles, we just want to make sure you stay put here," Reverend Sykes explained knowingly. "This is a tough neighborhood. Your neighbors give some pretty tough stares. We'll be staying with you tonight."

"Have any neighbors spoken to you yet?" Miss Daisy asked.

"No, ma'am. The moving truck unloaded at ten o'clock this morning. A crowd of neighbors gathered around the house talking, but no one said nothin' to us yet," his wife said as she entered the living room with a five-year-old tugging at her red plaid skirt. "Hello, I'm Maisie and this is our son, Chris," She extended her hand to Miss Daisy and Reverend Sykes.

"Nice to meet you," Miss Daisy smiled.

"Sorry about the mess. We'll try to make you as comfortable as possible under the circumstances," Maisie grinned. "I've prepared dinner. Come get a bite to eat."

After dinner, Miles proudly escorted Miss Daisy and Reverend Sykes through the house. "It's a beauty, isn't it?" Miles asked, opening a bedroom door. "This will be our room. It's stuffed with boxes now, but with some fixin up here and there, it will be grand."

Suddenly, a brick burst through the front window, sending a flood of shattered glass into the living room. A stack of books crashed to the floor.

Adrenalin pumped. Miles and Reverend Sykes ran downstairs to the living room window. A mob of over one hundred white neighbors hurled insults, stones, and bricks. Miss Daisy, Chris, and Maisie huddled in the corner beneath a table. Miss Daisy's arm shielded the little boy from the broken glass. Chris sobbed. Maisie rocked him gently. "Hush, baby," Maisie whispered. "Hush."

Miss Daisy trembled. She felt helpless. It was her first time witnessing the horrifying sounds of an angry mob in action. "Reverend, can we go out and stop them?" Miss Daisy asked as she crept on her knees to the window.

Reverend Sykes's eyes moved from her frightened face to the darkness of the window. "I don't think that many angry people will listen," he said. "Why don't you grab the phone and call the police. It's too dangerous for us out there."

Miss Daisy crawled to the kitchen, calling the police. Her eyes flitted about the room as she returned beneath the table with Maisie and Chris. "I called the police," she screamed. "They're on their way now."

"Thank you, Jesus," Maisie whispered, kissing Chris's forehead.

Miles's arms grew limp at his sides. He remained paralyzed against a wall. "It's no use," he said, shaking his head. "How we goin to stay here? We're goin to die!"

Reverend Sykes took his arm. "No, it's time to fight. It's not time to give up. You aren't slaves anymore," he shouted bitterly. "You bought this house. This is your house. This is your country. Stand up and fight for what is yours!"

Clutching his cross in his fists, Reverend Sykes charged through the front door outside beneath the single yellow light bulb on the porch. "This is a peaceful residence," he cried. "Go to your homes, we've called the police."

But the mob did not listen. Harsh voices seared the air. Obscure faces muddled in darkness hurled more insults. The noise of the mob grew louder. At that moment, a police car drove up. Reverend Sykes waved them to the porch, but they remained at the back of the mob, idly watching the scene.

Reverend Sykes ran inside, peering through the front window. "I don't understand," he said. "The two officers are just standing there."

Miss Daisy looked outside. "I don't believe it. Why aren't they helping us?"

"These people are like quinine pills, Miss Daisy," Miles explained. "Sweet and nice on the outside and bitter tastin' on the inside. They don't care about us."

The house was pelted with more stones. Another brick crashed through a window. Maisie screamed. Chris whimpered. Miss Daisy, Miles, and Reverend Sykes buried themselves under the window. Gradually, the crowd dispersed. The house grew silent. There was a knock at the door.

Miss Daisy shuddered. "Are they coming inside for us now?" she asked, nervously.

Reverend Sykes's eyes narrowed like crescents. "Who is it?" he asked, uneasily.

"The police," a deep voice echoed. "Open up."

Miles opened the door. "Sir?" he questioned.

"You got a bit of a mess to clean up here," one officer said, smiling at the other officer. "Everyone is gone now."

Miles nodded.

"These people want to live here and they want no trouble," Miss Daisy complained.

"And we don't want any trouble neither," an officer said harshly. "It'd be just as well as you forget this night. There's not too much damage. Clean everything up and live quietly."

"Damage? Look at this damage!" Miss Daisy pointed. "This is their house!"

Reverend Sykes grabbed her arm. "Thank you, officers. We'll clean this up," he explained. "These people mean no harm. They just want a good place to live."

Miles nodded again and shut the door behind the officers.

Everyone peered through the gloom. All the windows were broken. Glass, stones, and bricks lay over the floors. The insults pained their psyche. Outside, their car was vandalized, the headlights and windshield shattered. Miles was devastated. He gave a heavy sigh. "Do we stay?"

Maisie stood up. "We stay," she said with a firm resolve.

"We'll do everything we can," Reverend Sykes added. "We can't stop now."

"We're here for you," Miss Daisy said, hugging Chris. "We're here for you. Things must change."

CHAPTER 22

There she was, hands clasped next to her heart, and a long flowing black dress standing next to a baby grand piano. In another photo trimmed in silver, Carmela Rossini played the piano, her platinum hair dyed black in a curly feminine hairdo, and she had heavy make-up and a seductive glow in her eyes.

Scattered above the worn-out upright in her living room were several black and white photographs from Mrs. Rossini's old days performing in small opera houses in Italy.

Mrs. Rossini's Lytle Street apartment was a temple of her past. The house, located next door to Ida's friend Florence, had a warm and pleasant atmosphere. The living room was moss green, enhanced by black furniture, and a dark green sofa and chair, like sinking ships, were slightly torn.

In one photo, Mrs. Rossini and her eleven-year-old daughter, Tina, looked alike, with hair pressed and curled, their faces aligned in dark silhouette. "Mama, I want to be like you," said Tina, now eighteen, as she looked at the photographs. "I want to perform in New York one day."

Sitting sideways at her desk and leaning on her elbow, Mrs. Rossini spoke slowly and cautiously between drags of her cigarette. "Everyone in Europe worships Radio City," she said in an Italian accent as thick as the day she arrived at Ellis Island seven years ago. "With much practice and luck you can get there, dear Tina." She stopped for a moment, taking the last drag from her cigarette, holding her breath while grinding the cigarette into the silver ashtray. Then she allowed the smoke to bellow out of her mouth through pursed lips.

Tina sighed as she fell back on the couch, carefully placing her feet on the coffee table crowded with knick-knacks from Italy. "Practice and discipline," she said. "And more practice."

Mother and daughter came to New York shortly after World War II when there was nothing left for them in Italy. Tina's father, a Jewish cellist from Genoa, died of a heart attack seven years earlier and the Holocaust had taken many other relatives. With three small suitcases filled with clothes and mementos, Mrs. Rossini and Tina boarded a large ship headed for America.

Passenger liners tooted and fireboats greeted new immigrants with sprays of water against the partly cloudy sky of New York Harbor. People gasped, pointed, and crowded the decks to get a glimpse of the Statue of Liberty. Mrs. Rossini held Tina's hand tightly as she made her way through the shoulders of old women grasping the rails. Her dark eyes stared at the tips of the Statue's green crown and a slither of a rainbow disappeared in the passing gray clouds.

On Ellis Island, immigrants were herded into a gray stone and red brick warehouse where they were given showers, tagged, and abused by the authorities. As they waited in holding pens, officials tore husbands away from wives, children away from parents, and brothers away from sisters. They changed names they could not pronounce. Old people and those who looked like bums were returned to their native homes and the sick were quarantined. Mrs. Rossini and Tina clung to each other, sitting on the bare wooden benches in the waiting pen, wondering what fate would befall them.

Mrs. Rossini vividly recalled those days at Ellis Island. Although the experiences were new and frightening, Mrs. Rossini believed their immigration to the United States would reap due rewards through the success of Tina's budding singing career. She laughed nervously now and leaned back against the living room chair. Calm and cool in her long green dress, she appeared worn. Her lifetime of discipline and hardship was seen in her expression and heard in the roughness of her voice.

Tina's motivation, the gift of her voice, and the dreams of her mother were a wonderful combination for hope, but not a guarantee of success. "Sometimes I feel so close," Tina said softly as she looked at another photograph atop the piano.

"Sometimes is not enough," Mrs. Rossini said bluntly. "It's time to practice now, you must sing at Dorotea's House tomorrow evening and for Miss Daisy at the Rosedale mansion Saturday. It should be a lovely event and wonderful opportunity. You never know who will be there. You just never know."

CHAPTER 23

The following evening at Dorotea's House, "the Club" and center of activity for the Italian community in Princeton, Tina's fear mounted as she waited to appear on stage. Despite the heavy mascara, painted ruby red lipstick, make-up, and elegant black floor-length gown, she felt translucent like ice, afraid the audience may detect her fear.

As the lights were raised, Tina gracefully walked across the small stage, her eyes widening for dramatic effect while she raised her slender arm to greet the audience applause. With the hush of silence in the darkness, she bellowed notes of an Italian love song. Music filled her body and resonated throughout the hall, echoing a melody of lost love. Tina imagined, in the audience, rows upon rows of people at Radio City in New York. At the climax of her song, the audience applauded and quieted again, in anticipation of the suspenseful and sustained last note.

Suddenly, thunderous applause rushed through Dorotea's house, shaking the wooden floors. Tina nodded and bowed to the exuberant standing ovation of the audience.

Mrs. Rossini waited behind the curtain. Her applause was intense with excitement. "Brava!" she shouted with tears. "Brava, what a performance! The best you've ever had!"

Tina hugged her mother tightly, weeping. "I was so scared. I thought I wouldn't be able to sing, but I thought about Radio City. I believed I was there and it all came out."

"I knew you had it in you." Mrs. Rossini kissed Tina on her forehead. "Now there's someone here who wants to meet you," she said, holding her daughter's face in her wrinkled hands.

Tina wiped the tears from her eyes and peered over her mother's shoulders into the shadows. "Who, Mama? Who wants to meet me, an agent? Was an agent here?" Tina asked in a high voice.

"No, Tina. A very nice gentleman. Professor Anthony Florentino. A professor of English from the university," Mrs. Rossini beckoned with her hand.

A tall man, with a broad face and gentle smile, stepped from the darkness into the light. He wore a black double-breasted suit with a vest and plain tie. "Miss Tina, you sang beautifully. What an honor it is to meet you," he said, looking at Tina with a flash of his dark brown eyes.

Tina was struck by the golden highlights in his brown hair, which though thinning, caught the stage lights in beautiful shimmers. His twinkling eyes, framed by long curly lashes, searched hers.

"Thank you," she said shyly.

"My name is Anthony Florentino. I teach English at the university," he started.

Tina smiled. "Oh, the university. It must be a wonderful job."

"It is very interesting. I usually have such a busy schedule, but I'm happy I took the evening to come here and listen to your beautiful song," Anthony continued.

"I'm glad you enjoyed it. It takes so many hours of practice and it's gone in a flash on stage," Tina said, fidgeting with her hands.

"It would be an honor to take you to dinner," Anthony said reluctantly and giggled. "Are you available tomorrow evening?"

Tina looked away and shrugged in embarrassment. "I'm so sorry. I would love to, but I have another singing engagement tomorrow evening at Rosedale for Miss Daisy."

"How about six at Lahiere's Restaurant? It's a few hours earlier. I won't keep you late. I promise," Anthony persisted, playing with his tie, revealing a childlike anxiety.

Tina glanced at her mother. Mrs. Rossini nodded with approval.

"All right. I must be on time for Miss Daisy's event," Tina warned. "I must get there no later than seven-thirty. This could be my big chance. There will be agents from the theaters in Trenton and New York."

Anthony smiled. "I know that must be exciting. I appreciate you taking the time for me. Thank you. I look forward to having dinner with you. Here's my office number. Call me when you're ready to be picked up."

Tina nodded graciously.

Anthony disappeared into the shadows of the audience.

"He's so handsome," Mrs. Rossini said.

"Mama, are you setting me up?" Tina asked, placing her hands on her hips.

"No, I never met him until this evening," Mrs. Rossini explained. "He watched your performance beside me and asked if I knew you."

"And of course you had to tell him you were my mother and my whole life story," Tina smirked.

"No, dear. I talked about you a bit, but he wanted to hear you sing."

"Are you sure he's not an agent?"

"You see for yourself on his business card, he's with the university's English department," Mrs. Rossini said, lighting a cigarette.

Tina looked at the small card in her hands. "It does say Princeton University."

Mrs. Rossini blew smoke from her tightly pursed red lips. "This is good, Tina," she said.

"Maybe. He is quite handsome," Tina giggled.

"Tina," Mrs. Rossini said, hugging her daughter. "This is a wonderful evening for you. A wonderful performance and a wonderful young man. A Princeton University professor no less. This may be your chance, Tina. What blessings," she said, kissing her. "America's filled with dreams."

CHAPTER 24

From Witherspoon Street, Lahiere's Restaurant looked so cozy nestled between two shops, it was almost impossible not to be drawn into its large dining area with romantic light. Once inside, there were displays of tapas with garlic shrimp in sherry vinegar and marinated anchovies near the bar and a pungent display of cheeses, alluringly arrayed at the front.

Anthony and Tina sat in a dim corner by candlelight. Waiters in black tie strolled between crowded tables. Tina sipped wine with a plate of calamari and casserole of clams steamed with mushrooms. Anthony finished trout fillet, served on a bed of spinach dotted with bacon bits.

"There's so many questions I have," Tina giggled, "But now that I'm with you, I can't remember any of them."

Anthony gently wiped his mouth. "You've asked many of the common questions," he said. "You know I was born here in America. I'm twenty-eight years old. My parents are from Italy. I teach English. I love my job. I'm very busy with my job. There's not so much to tell. But you, Tina. You seem to have a magnificent future."

"I don't have an agent yet," Tina sighed. "That's the key and I need a wonderful agent in New York. That will get me to the place I want."

"And marriage?" Anthony asked, arching his left eyebrow.

Tina looked puzzled. "Marriage?"

"It doesn't seem like you will have room for marriage and a family with such a budding singing career," Anthony said, leaning forward.

Tina fumbled with her fork. "I'm busy like you are. I practice many hours a day. I have many auditions. I don't have anyone in mind now," she explained. "I would definitely make time to date someone if I found the right gentleman."

Anthony hesitated. "That's good to hear. You're such a beautiful woman. I'm in love with your accent. It's ever so slight," Anthony smiled. "It would be a waste not to find the right gentleman."

Tina averted his gaze. "Thank you for such a wonderful evening," she began. "I must go now."

"We must do it again soon," Anthony added. "Won't you have dessert? A cookie or rice pudding?"

"I'd love to, but I don't want to be late to Rosedale," Tina said, looking around the restaurant. "I'm glad we made our date earlier at five. It's a little after six now. I really think it's time to go to Rosedale. Will you be staying to hear me sing?" Tina sat up in her chair.

"Oh, I have so much work. Research. There's always research. I'm sorry, Tina. I just managed to get this small precious moment with you. But I'd love to spend some more time with you." He placed his large hand on top of hers.

Tina shifted on her chair. "And marriage for you? You seem busier than I am," she said sarcastically.

His eyes darted around the room. "Ahh, marriage. Marriage is wonderful if you can find the right woman," he said irritably, then seeing her hurt face, smiled.

"But don't you need to take the time to get to know the right woman?" Tina leaned forward with her elbow on the table.

"Yes, yes," Anthony said nervously. "Stop by my office at the university next Friday after four. I'll be working, but I'll take a few moments to see you. I'm very interested and want to learn more about you."

Tina looked down. "That's good. I'd like to see you again too. I'll be there at four. I hope I can find it."

"I'll call you at home first and give you directions. It's easy. You won't get lost."

"Oh, Anthony. It would mean so much if you came to Rosedale this evening." Tina pleaded.

"I know, but it's not convenient. I'll be there in spirit," Anthony said, kissing her hand.

"I must go. Can you take me to Rosedale?" Tina asked.

"Certainly. You'll do well, Tina. Maybe the agent you need will be there."

"I hope so," Tina muttered. "I certainly hope so."

Tina rushed from Anthony's automobile past the dexterous swirl of columns outside Rosedale. She entered the foyer and was escorted into a small waiting area where she caught her breath and freshened up a bit before being taken on the long walk upstairs. The large formal room, crowded with guests, spoke with Miss Daisy's voice and charisma. There was the triumphant blending of paneled walls, mantelpieces, odd bits of marble, and Genoese velvets. The paintings were animated by the small persistent sparkle of gold leaves and the painted furniture added a delicate mischief.

On this pleasant summer evening, muted white light from the sunset filtered through the windows. The reception room had footlights and the perfection of light on a small stage designed for Rosedale's entertainment. Three fiddlers, one accordionist, and rhythm musicians from Budapest, dressed in bright ties and gray sports coats, played. They dazzled the house with their wild energy. Tina listened and swayed with the music.

Someone tapped Tina from behind. A woman with a thick Italian accent spoke. "Tina, I was hoping you were here," Mrs. Rossini said, hugging her. "How was dinner?"

"Nice, Mama," Tina smiled.

"This is Miss Daisy, the owner of Rosedale," Mrs. Rossini said, pointing to the elderly woman next to her.

Miss Daisy, dressed in an elegant black gown, slumped over her cane. "I'm so happy you will sing. Everyone tells me so much about you. You're a very talented young lady. You'll go far," she said.

"Nice to meet you," Tina nodded. "Thank you for having me."

"You're due to go on after these gentlemen," Mrs. Rossini said. "Go on, make your way up front and wait there." Mrs. Rossini nodded.

"Yes, Mama," Tina said as she disappeared into the crowd.

When the applause for the gypsy musicians stopped, Tina stepped into the spotlight. She recoiled a bit as the glare hit her, flinching and raising her hand to shade her face. Wearing a strapless blue gown, her eyes shimmered with excitement. She sang Bizet's *Carmen*. Her voice was earthy and dusky. Though the first top notes quivered, she maintained considerable power and a soft sustaining melody. Tina had the strikingly attractive stage presence of a singer who carried audience attention from the first note to the last. Her song ended. The applause burst throughout the room. Tina bowed graciously, leaving the stage to find her mother.

As the next singer took centerstage, people nodded in silent approval as Tina made her way through the crowd. "Wonderful, Tina," her mother hugged her. "Excellent. Miss Daisy is in awe of you."

"Really?" Tina's eyes sparkled. "Any agents?"

"One," Mrs. Rossini whispered. "When you were singing, Miss Daisy introduced me to a New York agent named Thomas Arnold. I don't know where he went now, but he seemed impressed. He gave me his business card."

"Do we call him? When do we go to New York?" Tina asked excitedly.

"He asked for our number. He said he doesn't take calls, but he will call us Monday to set up an appointment," Mrs. Rossini explained.

"Oh, Mama. This is it! This is it!" Tina cried.

"You had a wonderful performance," Mrs. Rossini smiled. "Miss Daisy would like to have you sing again for her."

Tina nodded. "Why, of course."

Her mother's eyes widened. "And dinner? How was dinner? How was the gentleman?"

"He was very nice, Mama. I wish he could be here. He's so busy."

"And will you see him again?" Mrs. Rossini said, grabbing her forearm.

"Yes, Mama. Next Friday," Tina explained.

Mrs. Rossini nodded. "This is very good, Tina," she said, kissing Tina on the cheek. "Very, very good!"

CHAPTER 25

I t suits an intellect that ventures in a hundred directions, this painting in Anthony's small office in the English Department of Princeton University. It was a trompe l'oeil that showed two shelves with books from the early twentieth century. The rest of his office was simple and cold with the exception of two framed awards and an old Oxford University postcard taped on a white wall. The room lacked light and was dimmed with age. The wooden floors, in need of polish, were bare. Anthony sat at his cluttered desk covered with scattered white papers and newsprint, drinking coffee while madly scribbling words.

"Excuse me," Tina whispered, entering the office.

Anthony looked up. "Tina, how good to see you. It's four already?"

Tina nodded. "I love the painting," she smiled.

The scruffily handsome man whirled around to point to the work that animated the passions he was spinning out. "I get much of my inspiration from this painting," he explained. "It took much for this artist to put the painting together just as much as it takes much work to put together any good piece of literature." He rocked back and forth in his chair.

"How are you?" Tina asked.

"Fine, fine. Take a seat. It's the only seat I have in this small place. Care for some coffee?"

"Yes, please," Tina said, sitting in the chair.

"One minute," Anthony said, rising quickly from his chair. He walked down the hall into a small kitchen with a stove to pour coffee.

"You seem very busy. Are you sure I'm not imposing today?" Tina shouted down the hallway while untying her pink bonnet.

"No, it's quite all right. One moment, I'll be right there," he said, carrying two cups of coffee into the office.

"There. I hope you like it black. There's no cream left," Anthony smiled.

"Yes, black is fine."

"I need a break. I've been working hard all day."

"Is your work difficult?" Tina asked, leaning her elbow on the desk. "I see a few certificates and awards. You seem accomplished already."

"Sometimes. Sometimes it's difficult." Anthony took a sip of coffee. He explained publication in literary magazines almost immediately upon arrival to the university, the winning of prestigious prizes, and receiving invitations to read. "Sometimes public attention makes it more difficult to write. People always expect more out of you. Really, though, I think I've been lucky."

"Do you teach many courses here?"

Anthony swiveled in his chair. "I teach literature and at least two writing courses."

Tina looked impressed. "It seems to be much to do."

"I'm always working hard and had much domestic business that caused much tension in the last few years. Sometimes it's hard to think, you know?" He leaned forward, sipping coffee.

"Domestic business?" Tina asked.

"It's a long story. I don't want to bore you.

"What about your students? What are they like?"

As he ran through descriptions of his students, he wrapped his hand around his coffee cup. "I could keep telling you stories about them. Some are insightful and others . . . I wonder how they have reached the university level," he chuckled.

Tina giggled. "My life has been busy with singing practice. I was disappointed this week. We met an agent at Rosedale, but he never bothered to call. Mama tried calling several times, but we got no answer." She paused. "I hate moments like these. I think I'm so close, but in reality my dreams seem so far away. Agents tell you they will call and they never do. It's hard to trust and depend on these men, do you understand?"

Tina sat back in the chair, the determined high pitched voice echoed through the hallway. She tried catching her breath because she was speaking passionately and fast.

"It's hard, I know. But you're good, Tina. If you keep trying, you're bound to get there." Anthony gazed into her eyes.

"But you've only heard me sing once," Tina said. "I wish you could hear me again and really tell me if I have a chance."

"When are you singing again?"

"Mama has been making more arrangements. I'll let you know."

"And I'll be there," Anthony smiled. "Do you like cup custard?"

"Yes, I love it."

"What are you doing tomorrow at noon?"

"Nothing but practice. And more practice. You know Mama," Tina sighed.

"Meet me here tomorrow at noon. I'll take you out for cup custard. I'm sorry I'm swamped today. I have much work to do as usual, but I want to see you again," Anthony said, kissing her on her cheek.

Tina blushed. "I look forward to seeing you again," she smiled, gently stroking her cheek as she left his office.

CHAPTER 26

The soft white custard had the texture of over-whipped cream. It gave gently when the spoon dipped into the cup. It was cold and savory, slightly sweet. The most lovable food imaginable. Tina licked the bottom of her spoon and scraped the custard cup. Anthony, sitting on the bench under the trees in the courtyard, placed his arm around her, smiling. He knew this was Tina's most favorite and delightful treat.

"Tell me more about you, Anthony," Tina giggled.

"What more do you need to know?" Anthony smiled.

"Not much more. Do you live around here? I suppose you do," she said.

"Yes, I live close by. Most of the professors live near campus," he answered.

Tina's eyes penetrated his. "So, is it an apartment? Do you rent it? Is it a house? How big is it?"

"Wait a minute! You've asked too many questions," Anthony chuckled.

Tina folded her arms across her chest. "Now you have a chance to answer them."

"I have a house. It's a small house, though. Three bedrooms, living room, dining room, you know what I mean," Anthony began.

"That doesn't sound too small to me," Tina smirked. "Take me there. I'd love to see it. It must be beautiful."

"Far from the truth," Anthony stared at the ground. "It's a bachelor's house. All simple. No decorating. Not much furniture. A lot has to be done with it before I have you over."

"I won't laugh, I promise," Tina said, standing. She grabbed his left arm and tugged. "Please, let's go. I'd love to see where you live. I'm sure it's not that bad."

"It's that bad, Tina," Anthony explained, pulling her to the bench. "I'll show it to you soon. Just give me some time to clean it up a bit. I don't want you to stop seeing me because I'm such a slob."

"All right. But I want to see your house soon," Tina warned.

"Let's go for a walk on the campus. Do you walk on campus often?" Anthony asked.

"Hardly. I don't ever seem to have the time. Mama wants me to practice," Tina muttered. "She says I don't practice enough. I'm surprised she's letting me have some time to see you."

"I'm glad she lets you see me."

"I'm happy too, but I wish I could have more time."

"Ah, time. Everyone needs more time."

"There never seems to be enough of it to go around."

"Never."

A silence gathered as they walked beneath the ancient trees on campus. The wind lifted suddenly and blew aside clouds. A splash of sun cascaded across the blue sky.

"Let's sit here," Anthony suggested. "This is my favorite place. I like to read or rest here on this lawn. It's so peaceful. The stone buildings look like fortresses, don't they?"

"I guess," Tina said, sitting beside him on the grass. "It is peaceful and quiet."

"And no people. No professors. No students."

"No one."

Anthony closed his eyes with his face toward the sun. "Doesn't the warmth of the sun feel good?"

Tina paused. She watched as he opened his eyes again to look at her. Strong passion lanced her eyes. His hand beckoned her closer. Anthony caressed her face. "You're so beautiful," he spoke softly.

Tina looked down. Then she lifted her head after a time. "Thank you."

Anthony turned and leaned over, his body spreading warmth into her. His mouth pressed hard against her lips. Tina opened her mouth and embraced him. He gently unbuttoned her blouse, exposing her breasts.

"You're so beautiful, Tina," he whispered, cupping them with his hands.

Her eyes lifted to his in passion. She touched his face, then his hair. Tina lay open as he rhythmically thrust inside. The sky swirled. She moaned. Then a long shudder. They lay as lovers, sharing a peaceful exhaustion. Slowly, the world came into focus again. His eyes gently peered down at her. "Tina, that was beautiful," Anthony said tenderly.

Tina sat up, her legs drawn up under her skirt. She nodded.

"Was that your first time?" he asked.

Tina nodded again. Anthony kissed her again. "It was beautiful, Tina. You are beautiful. I want you in my life," he said, caressing her face.

Anthony held her hand. "I'll walk you home."

Tina looked deep in his dark brown eyes and leaned against his shoulder. "Thank you, Anthony."

"Will you see me again? I'd love to spend forever with you," Anthony said as they walked toward Nassau Street.

"Of course," Tina smiled. "I'd love to see you again. I like being with you."

Anthony chuckled. "I like being with you too. Come visit me at the office again next week. We'll go out for cup custard again."

"I'd love that," Tina giggled.

Anthony stopped to kiss her again. "Come and visit with me every Friday."

Tina looked at her watch. "Oh no, Mama," she shouted. "She's been waiting for me. I forgot my practice with her. We'd better hurry."

CHAPTER 27

It was Guy Bartels, Miss Daisy's cousin from Charleston, who tipped Tina off about auditions for young singers in New York. Tina showed up two hours early on a Sunday afternoon, the first of sixty who tried out for an intermission spot onstage in a small theater on the west side of Manhattan.

The event was thrilling and terrifying. Overall, the singers seemed to thrive. Each performed two arias, one in the morning and one in the afternoon. Not surprisingly, most were more relaxed after lunch.

The contestants had admirable qualities, although some needed more development. Edward Browne, a countertenor from Philadelphia, was the oldest singer to audition at twenty-nine. Janine Petersburg, a twenty-three-year-old from Connecticut, was not very solid in her arias. Peter Brushkov, a twenty-five-year-old tenor from Florida, displayed an immature pliant voice in the familiar aria by Donzinetti. Carmen Santanilla, a twenty-two-year-old soprano from New York, sang with a warm lustrous voice, with some unsteadiness. Tina, now a twenty-one-year-old mezzo soprano, brought zest and bright sound to an excerpt from Strauss's "Ariadne and Naxos," then revealed her musical depth in an aria called "Vanessa."

Everyone waited in the backstage area until late evening for the announcement of winners. It was a cold, institutional-looking place with corridors of black and white tile and gray metal lockers. Edward seemed calm, taking a drag from his cigarette. Peter paced the floor beneath the dim electric lights. Janine complained about the audition. Carmen cried alone in the corner. Tina fidgeted with her fingernails in anticipation.

A tall blonde woman in a long black gown taped the names on the dressing room bulletin board. Everyone huddled. One by one, each singer left the board in dismay. Edward Browne won the top spot for the men. Tina had won the top spot for the women. Each was scheduled for several appearances the following month.

Tina was in ecstasy. She hugged and kissed Edward. She whirled about, dancing with Janine. Tina ran to the nearest pay phone outside the theater and called her mother who was equally excited. Then she dialed Anthony at his university office, hoping he was working late.

"Hello," a deep voice answered.

"Anthony, Anthony," Tina began. "I got it! I made it! I'll be singing in the intermission spots in New York."

"Wonderful, Tina. I'm so happy," Anthony said with an encouraging voice.

"I start this weekend! Can you believe it! This weekend! Please tell me you'll come see me. I've called Mama, and she's coming and some of our friends will . . . " she shouted.

"I can't, love. I'm sorry," Anthony explained.

Tina paused. "Anthony, you heard me sing over three years ago at Dorotea's House. You've never heard me since.

I thought you loved me. I thought you cared about what I do. I thought we'd be getting married one day."

"I love you, Tina. It just takes so much to get out of this office. I hope you understand," Anthony pleaded.

"No, I don't understand. How can you love me if you can't come and see what I do best? You don't seem to be interested," Tina cried irritably.

"I am interested, Tina. Listen to me," Anthony spoke softly. "I am very happy for you. This is the best news. I'll make it to one of your performances soon. I promise. I'm sure you'll be having more and more each day. Honey, I love you. Congratulations, love."

Tina paused. "Thanks, Anthony. Just a thought, I don't know if I'll get to see you this week. I must buy a new gown or two and . . ."

"Don't worry. Do what you need. Call me and let me know how you're doing. We'll make the time to see each other like we always have. Good-bye, love," Anthony whispered.

"Good-bye," Tina said sadly, placing the phone on the receiver.

Tina's intermission spots were received with so much enthusiasm that Mrs. Rossini secured an agent to help with finances and events. Soon Tina was booked at other theaters and supper clubs in the city. Her commutes from Princeton to downtown Manhattan increased in frequency. She woke up at four-thirty in the morning, ate breakfast, and took the long train ride into the city for professional voice lessons, rehearsals, and evening performances. Most evenings, she did not return to Princeton until midnight.

Tina spent much of her time in the cluttered dressing rooms of theaters. A small cot, long rectangular table, and several chairs furnished the room. Each chair, opposite a lighted mirror, had white counter space for dancers, singers, and performers for meals and doing hair and make-up. Her area was the smallest and neatest, with miniature straw baskets for make-up and hair pins. Two photographs, one of Anthony, the other of her mother, hung on the bare wall next to a light bulb. A timer was placed on the wooden shelf below the counter to wake her between rehearsals and performances.

Tina tried to maintain her relationship with mother and Anthony in Princeton, seeing them for a few hours during the week, but it became difficult. Tina was so fatigued from her busy schedule that she decided to stay in a small hotel room in Brooklyn for three to four nights at a time. The hotel room was shabby, decorated in dingy golds and browns, and traffic noise screeched through one tiny window, but Tina did not mind because she could get some sleep. Although she begged Anthony to come visit, he politely refused, complaining about his lack of time for adequate research and overly scheduled student appointments.

Tina finally rented a room on the tenth floor of an apartment building, closer to the theater district, on 72nd Street and Broadway. She lived in a two-bedroom apartment with an eighty-year-old retired teacher she met through her singing instructor. The new arrangement made it easier to attend rehearsals, voice lessons, and performances with adequate rest.

CHAPTER 28

On a crisp, clear autumn afternoon in September 1956, Tina made a surprise visit to Anthony's office at the university. The gentle wind blew colored leaves across her path as she walked across large green lawns. As she approached his office building, she caught a glimpse of a couple embracing, leaning against the ivy-laced stone wall. Tina smiled, thinking about Anthony. She looked down at the ground and quickly looked up again, recognizing the man engaged in a full, deep kiss. Tina hesitated, then gulped. "Anthony?" she whispered. She fidgeted nervously with her hands. "Anthony?"

The woman with long blonde hair and rosy cheeks turned around quickly. "Oh, my," she started. "Anthony, I told you we shouldn't do this here. One of your students is bound to catch us. I'm sorry, dear. Would you like to speak with my husband? I don't often get much time to see him. I'm so ashamed of our public display of affection."

Tina paused, lifting her face into the sunlight as the wind tugged at her orange flowered dress.

"Tina, Tina," Anthony said, his voice quivering a bit. "Step into my office. I know you need to pick up your brother's paper. I have a few moments."

"Married?" Tina asked abruptly. "This is your wife?"

The silence was ominous.

"Oh, dear," the woman giggled. "Anthony, you never tell your students and their friends we are married, do you? Maybe the subject just doesn't come up."

He stared gloomily at the ground. "No, it doesn't," Anthony said, placing his hands in his pockets.

Tina's breath broke into harsh gasps over her terrified face. "Ma'am, have you been married a long time?" she asked softly.

"Why, yes for at least ten years now. Our eleventh anniversary is next month. And if you'd like to know, we're expecting our first child in January, isn't that exciting?" the woman said, placing her hand on her stomach. "I'm flattered you like my husband so much. The professors say he is very well liked by the young people."

Anthony adverted Tina's glare. "Meredith, please go now. I know Tina must pick up her brother's paper and it's quite important that I discuss some of the corrections on this paper now. We wouldn't want her brother to get a bad grade, would we?" Anthony lied, shifting from side to side. His arms reached out toward Tina.

"That's all right," Tina stuttered. "That's all right. My brother will get his own paper. I shouldn't have come here in the first place for him. He probably won't be in class anymore, Anthony. That's what I came to tell you. He won't be back in class."

"What?" Anthony asked, wiping the sweat from his brow. "Now just take a few moments, come into my office and we'll talk."

They stood in astonished silence. Anthony looked at Tina anxiously.

Tina wiped the tears from her face. "No!" she shouted. "He told me to tell you that he hated your class. He hates you. He told me to tell you you're a lousy professor. You don't care about your students. You don't care about him. You don't care about anyone, but yourself! You're a liar, Professor Florentino! A cheat! Am I making myself clear? You're the biggest liar! And my brother told me to make sure I tell you he is never coming back!" Tina turned and ran across the university's green lawns onto Nassau Street.

The crowd converged upon the doors of the train headed for New York. Tina slipped through clouds of hissing steam into the third car. She wanted to get away from Princeton. Far away. Meredith's voice haunted her. Rage and disappointment swelled up in the pit of her stomach like a volcano on the brink of eruption. She discreetly wiped tears from her face, trying to maintain composure.

Upon arrival in the city, Tina boarded an unfamiliar street car. She did not care where it was headed. Deciding she had ridden long enough, Tina got off at a dark corner near a saloon in a crowded tenement. Inside, she drank and sobbed uncontrollably.

Afterwards, she walked the streets with its ash barrels and dirt, like a vagabond, looking aimlessly through store windows and avoiding eye contact with those who passed. Rasping poverty engulfed her. Prostitutes on street corners made deals with well-dressed business men. Drunkards pissed on the apex of hydrants. The stench of urine-smothered babies. Tina overheard the shouts of grown-ups and cries of children, hidden behind dark tenement facades, taking blows and curses for dinner.

Tina had never seen this side of New York, a barren wasteland gripped by raw winds and cold. Groups of young boys huddled on the streets. A scrawny gray cat, with belly sagging, sifted through garbage cans in the shadows. The graffiti and obscene drawings painted on sides of tenement walls: a swastika, endless faces, repetitive letters and initials in lover's hearts crossed out made her weep.

Tina was suddenly drowned in a deluge of noise from the streets. She stumbled her way through Printing House Square. The neighborhood roared with presses, spinning words of the past upon rolls of white paper. Her mind spun out of control in the alley; a young woman without the powerful lyrics of a song, and the courage that brought her to this point in life, collapsed.

Waiting for another streetcar, she thought about dying beneath its wheels. Tina watched several trolleys start, swerve, screech with bells ringing, and stop before her as she held the lamp post like a man around the waist, swirling in the golden dust of the street light.

An old woman, wrapped in a ragged black cloak, tapped Tina on the shoulder. "It gets awfully cold out here," she said in a low gruff voice. "I have an apartment upstairs where it's warm. Please come inside."

The old woman was gentle. She led Tina into a tiny apartment like a broom closet, and shared a cup of tea. The old woman listened. She finally convinced Tina to go home and put her on a trolley.

The next day, there was a strong breeze blowing off the bay and the afternoon sun beamed on the promenade along the avenue. Men shouted, "Live lobsters! Come and get 'em!"

Across the pier, another man yelled to those passing by, "Fish. Get your fresh fish, here. Fish!" Other workers spread flounder and black fish across large tables, putting them in piles and piercing them with orange and white price tags. A boat, sounding its foghorn, appeared in the distance. Another old man called out, "More fish comin in! More fish comin in! It's fresh!"

Suddenly, people rushed in a half-run for a good place to inspect the catch of the day near the railing, bargaining with ship hands over prices.

Tina, hanging over the pier's metal rail, watched a man fillet a fish, throwing scraps in the air to seagulls. She missed morning rehearsal wandering about Sheepshead Bay, a weather-beaten fishing village of desolate race tracks and abandoned hotels. She tried to clear her mind.

Tina paced the piers, wondering how she could be deceived by Anthony for so long. She thought about life and her dreams as she walked home toward the trains. Tina sobbed, tasting salt tears. The sun sat blood red on the horizon and the breeze blew briskly cold.

CHAPTER 29

Lately, Tina was busy traveling the world singing her expanded repertory of operatic roles. The line to see a performance at the Metropolitan Opera on Saturday evening in April, 1964, spilled outside, winding along West 64th Street in a traffic-blocking mass of people. Though the theater was almost full, the crowd was reluctant to leave. The event was a showcase of the best opera singers from around the world.

Tina, with heavy make-up and wide brown eyes, stepped into the spotlight against a burlap backdrop. Special lighting on stage drew attention to her glamour. In her sleek, shimmering gown with her dark brown hair pulled back, she turned heads. The house lights dimmed. The crowd quieted. In a slow, dramatic tone, her voice rose. Tina began with beguiling melodies by Puccini. First, the lullaby "E Puccelino," then a cheerful love song "Sole e Amore." She followed with Stravinsky's "Baba the Turk." Then Tina ended her performance with two Negro spirituals she used to hear echo from the churches in her Princeton neighborhood on Lytle and Witherspoon Streets. She intrigued the audience with her masterful and down-home delivery of "Every Time I Feel the Spirit" and "Git on Board."

Applause filled the room, cameras flashed. The audience gave a standing ovation. Tina stood centerstage, bowing and smiling. She was ebullient, blowing kisses to the crowd. Mrs. Rossini applauded feverishly.

Mrs. Rossini met Tina backstage with a hug. "I'm so proud!" she cried. "I knew you'd make the big time. I knew it!"

Tina cried in her mother's arms. "It was the most triumphant feeling, Mama. All the practice, all the sacrifice and hard work were worth it. I can't believe I've made it here."

"It hasn't been easy."

"No, Mama. Not at all."

"But it was worth it! Believe it, Tina. Papa would be so proud," Mrs. Rossini said in her thick Italian accent.

"Mama, I want a picture. If it weren't for you, I wouldn't be here. Have my friend Melissa take our picture together," Tina said, pointing to a short, blonde woman behind them. "Melissa, please take our picture."

Melissa took the camera from Mrs. Rossini, fumbling for a moment. "Smile," she said, focusing.

Mrs. Rossini and Tina pressed their heads together, their faces aligned in dark silhouette with a seductive glow in their eyes. The camera flashed. The color photo would be enlarged and framed in silver, placed on Mrs. Rossini's worn-out upright in her Princeton living room with other precious memories.

CHAPTER 30

Things were better by 1967. At least they appeared that way. Whites and colored people worked side by side in nearby factories. In downtown Princeton, colored folk worked as cashiers in the small shops on Nassau Street. Faces of white and colored children pressed against the counter of Pollies Fine Candies in Palmer Square, ogling for speckled jelly beans. White waiters served coloreds in restaurants. A few colored teachers taught in the public schools.

Time passed quickly. Miss Ida B., now a sixty-seven-year old woman, hardly recognized people in the town of Princeton anymore. The old sounds of blacksmith hammers with the tinkle of horse-car bells were silent. Stables and horse auctions had long ceased. The only two posts left standing for tying horses were found on John and Nassau Streets.

There were more houses, roads, businesses, and people. There were more transient families with separate lives, separate homes, separate telephones, and less stopping by to see how the neighbors were. The old community dwindled and changed. Jackson Street was demolished. Mr. Ball's Candy Store on John Street was now a residence. The Charcoal Inn, a meeting place and social club for the

Nemderoloc (colored men spelled backwards), was also deemed another residence. The Elks Home on MacClean Street moved to Birch Avenue. Miss Vann's Ice Cream Parlor, where Miss Ida B. used to buy ice cream with her friends at 165 Witherspoon Street, no longer existed.

Six hard back chairs sat empty against the light green wall on a porch on John Street. Many old friends had passed and moved away. Miss Ida B. wore black for a year. Her husband died from a heart attack in late 1964. Florence developed breast cancer, passing away in 1965. Beatrice lost her husband the same year, moving south to live with her children because Princeton rents were too high.

Mrs. Rossini, elderly and ailing, still lived on Lytle Street. She often shared stories with neighbors about her daughter's life. Tina, married with three children, had a successful opera career. She intended to move her mother into their new mansion in North Jersey the following month. Mrs. Rossini lamented the day she was due to leave the old community.

The Rosedale house, with its face watching history, stood majestically on Rosedale Road. Miss Daisy and Barker had long passed away, with property subdivided for new homes and changing the terrain of the valley.

These were Miss Ida B.'s thoughts as she walked along Nassau Street. It was all sad because the old neighborhood was a real place with love and character, but it had changed. Most children had grown up and left. Few remained because there was nothing to stay for.

Life was short. It seemed nothing more than a melody run out over the course of an era. On the other hand, life was precious. Miss Ida B. believed she was spared to keep an accounting, an oral history of sorts. Sometimes, life was like a three-stanza spiritual played in church on Sunday that lived eternally in her heart.

Suddenly, the wind blew Miss Ida B. toward a building. She rested near the lamp post for a moment to catch her breath. The winter sun set upon the horizon, a cold dark orb expanding into a night sky.

CHAPTER 31

Miss Ida B. heaved a great sigh. "All memories," she said sadly, walking inside from the balcony. "Nothing, but old memories now."

We stood in awe, wiping tears from our eyes. "It's amazing how one house weaves so many stories," I began.

"And to think my family is part of its legacy living here at Rosedale," Anna added, shaking her head from side to side. "Amazing."

Miss Ida B. crinkled her face pleasantly. "I've taken too long. I'm sorry we have to be at the cemetery," she reminded.

Anna called for Michaela from the playroom while escorting us to the front door. "Thank you for sharing your stories," Anna said kindly. "Please do come again. I'd love to hear more. You're welcomed at Rosedale anytime."

"Thank you for the playdate!" Michaela chirped.

"You're welcomed," Anna said, closing the front door.

Miss Ida B. looked at the face of Rosedale again. It stood in its usual grandeur. "That ol' house still whispers so many stories," she said, getting into the car.

The rain had stopped. Black clouds sifted through the skies. A gentle wind blew. We drove and parked the car on Quarry Street behind several black cars with black ribbons flying from their antennae. I helped Miss Ida B. from the car to the sidewalk. Michaela followed.

We walked along Witherspoon Street and entered the Princeton Cemetery, known as the "Westminster Abbey of the United States," and "the last resting place of noted men." We passed through rusted black iron gates to a place tucked away from the graves of Dean West, Cleveland, and Pyne. The colored section, on the north side, had its own entrance off Witherspoon Street.

Two large junipers draped over the pathway, separating the white section from the colored. The gravel crunched beneath our feet as we trudged under. An ancient oak, with small brown buds, gave birth to a few tiny green leaves. A robin skimmed the grass. The sweet smell of honeysuckle filled the air. Black squirrels scampered in decaying leaves beneath bushes.

There were two funerals today, one on the left side of the pathway and one on the right. On the left, the small group was meticulously dressed in dark suits and dresses. On the right, the same. Mourners wept. Their ministers prayed. Both grave sites, blanketed with a mass of flowers, lay in ominous silence. The soft breeze blew dandelion spores like white fur between the two gatherings. Bright sunlight cascaded across their faces. On the left, the faces were black. On the right, the faces were white.

Miss Ida B. closed her eyes to hide the tears, but they dripped down her dark cheeks. She quietly uttered "The Lord's Prayer." Kneeling beside the cement stone next to the fresh grave, she ran her wrinkled hand across the inscription of another close friend, "Beloved Mother, Patricia Harding, 1912–2000." Memories rose up and died in her mind. For a moment, the world withered away with long hurting thoughts and dead faces. The ghosts and shadows persisted, still divided even in death.

She wept as we walked, passing old tombstones with yellow dandelions pushed up beside them. Her tears fell and disintegrated along the path in the cemetery. Then spring rain fell as the sun shone. Twinkling drops danced upon the gravel. A clump of white posies in the colored section sparkled in a slither of sunlight. Miss Ida B. pointed to the sky. "The devil's beatin his wife," she whispered, wiping the tears with her white handkerchief. "The old people always told me, the devil is beatin his wife."

ABOUT THE AUTHOR

Dr. Donna L. Clovis is a graduate of Columbia University in New York City in journalism and the humanities. She has won a nomination for the Pulitzer Prize and a first-place feature-writing award for the National Association of Black Journalists. Dr. Clovis has also won two journalism fellowships: the McCloy Fellowship from the American Council on Germany and Harvard University and a Prudential Fellowship from Columbia University. She is also the Albert Einstein Education Award winner for achievements that produce a significant improved educational environment from the governor of New Jersey.

Dr. Clovis is interested in documentary work and storytelling that comes from this type of journalism. She especially loves talking with older people, to hear about their lives. This is the basis of her story and the synchronicity that occurred as she gathered the information through interviews and researching articles. It is called being in the right place at the right time. Dr. Clovis lives in the Princeton Junction area and loves to travel to other countries to learn more about people and culture.